# Cairns

**The Unity Church Journal of the Arts • Vol 13, 2021**

**Reredos Press**

Reredos Press • St. Paul, Minnesota

**Cairns: The Unity Church Journal of the Arts**
**Vol. 13, 2021, ©2021 by Unity Church-Unitarian**
ISBN 978-1-950996-04-9

**Reredos Press**

Published by Reredos Press
A program of Unity Church-Unitarian
732 Holly Ave., St. Paul, MN 55104
651-228-1456 / www.unityunitarian.org
Contact Us: cairns@unityunitarian.org

**Unity Church-Unitarian** is a free and inclusive, intergenerational congregation grounded in the heritage of liberal religion. Our shared ministry enlists the whole church family in living out the values of integrity, service, and joy at home, at church, and in the world.

My Hibiscus Tree                                                    Kathy Schur

# Contents

Cover
My Hibiscus Tree *Kathy Schur* (watercolor)

Departments

Features

*Foreword*
**Tired but Together**
**Marcia Franklin**
Cairns Co-editor

Unity Church-Unitarian, like most of the world, is having quite a year. We're navigating the tricky waters of COVID as best we can, striving to balance the needs of the congregation for community, support, and face-to-face togetherness against the sometimes-conflicting needs for public safety, caution, and peace of mind.

Meanwhile, we are simultaneously undergoing a completely normal, though nevertheless disruptive, time of ministerial transition. It's not that we're unprepared; we saw this transition coming. We just didn't see it coming quite like *this*. Given the unusual circumstances, we might be forgiven for wondering whether the measures in place to guide us through will be enough to get us to the other side unscathed.

We are all, in a word, tired.

And yet we "keep on keeping on." Some people have coped with the mental and spiritual fatigue by drawing or writing, others by cooking or sewing. I've made it this far with a now-weekly practice of baking café-sized muffins; binging Korean, Chinese, and Japanese dramas enough that I've started to pick up two new languages completely via immersion; and maintaining rigorous to-do lists that help me keep myself on task and each family member's schedule straight.

The techniques we each find don't necessarily refresh us for long, but they can help keep us from succumbing to the undertow that tugs at us so relentlessly, threatening to pull us under and overwhelm us—especially when we find ways to connect with each other.

While that pervasive feeling of exhaustion has come across clearly in the literary and visual art our contributors have shared with us this year, it is not the only theme. There are also many traces of hope.

Those traces come as splashes of color to brighten the mood, as Kathy Schur's cover image "My Hibiscus Tree" or Nancy Birger's "The Last Leaf" (p. 28). They come as reminders of what is *good* in our world and with each other—as in "Ode to a Goddess Yearning" by John David Wilson (p. 97) or "The Order of Things" by Daphne Thompson (p. 60)—or just a little "YIPPEE" from Richard Buggs in "Exuberance" (p. 78).

Sometimes our contributors ask us to acknowledge the pain of our times and the things that separate us from one another, like Mary E. Knatterud does in "COVID-Cut Ties" (p. 91) or Bill Quist in "Memorial Day" (p. 87). At other times, they remind us that two disparate ideas can peacefully co-exist in the same space, as in Robert Gestner's "Hong Kong 2" (p. 98), or as Molly Rodich shows us in "Window into the Soul" (p. 31), that what you see just depends on how you look at something.

Other contributors challenge us to re-examine our assumptions with pieces like "When Curiosity Becomes Faith" by Rebecca Gonzalez-Campoy (p. 36) or to take another, more deliberate look at the world around us as Joe Schur does in "ER" (p. 52). They help us to take ourselves less seriously with self-deprecating humor like in "Tales from My Un-Careers" by Kathryn Oakley (p. 64) or "Our Next Presenter" by Paul Englund (p. 29), and to find our way when we don't know where to turn, as Rev. Kathy Hurt does in "Lost" (p. 43).

Whether the message on the page is abstract, like "Peterson Family Spiral" by Beth Peterson (p. 35), straightforward like "Pomegranate, Kale, Wild Rice Salad" by Lisa Burke (p. 22), or somewhere in between, like the Art in Zoom presentation (beginning on p. 1), each and every contribution to *Cairns* came from a very personal place.

That our contributors are willing to share those pieces of themselves even now, when the world feels so overwhelming, speaks to the power of community. We may be tired, but we are *together*. I hope that you, too, can feel that togetherness, the embrace of our Beloved Community, here in the pages of *Cairns*.

## Art in Zoom
## Barbara Foss

On March 3, 2021, after a long season of cabin fever and winter grays as we observed COVID societal restrictions, missed seeing kith and kin, and longed for activities and worship at Unity Church, there was *Art in Zoom*.

Modeled after the annual event at many major art museums across the country called *Art in Bloom*, the Unity Art Team created a mini experience with a big impact. Using that good old connection-antidote for our many months of isolation Zoom, seven works of art were selected from Unity's collection (which numbers close to one hundred), and seven artists each volunteered to create a floral interpretation of one of the works. The art was hung in the Parish Hall; each floral artist installed their creation next to it, and Art Team member Paul Rogne, assisted by Unity staff member Madeline Summers, photographed each one.

Over 150 people from near and far signed on to Zoom for the special evening. Madeline made electronic magic, coordinating each floral artist speaking about their work while showing photos of the original artwork and the floral interpretation.

*Art in Zoom* was a great success—a visual feast that people will talk about for a long time.

Join us now on a colorful tour.

*Left: Unitarian Church in Transylvania* **by Zsolt Kovacs, floral artist Marla Simmet**
This painting depicts our partner church in Homoródszentpéter, Transylvania, which dates to 1526. Created by one of its members, it was gifted to Unity in 2010 to honor the strong relationship between the two congregations.

*Variations on a Circle* **by Rose Allen, floral artist Beth Black**
Previously, the piece has been part of the Minnesota Contemporary Quilters Challenge for projects on the theme, "Mélange a Trois." Created in 2015 and sold to Unity by the Evergreen Quilters, who support several local nonprofits with proceeds from sales.

*Fossil Blue* **by Munir Kahar, floral artist Dan Huelster**
Munir Kahar was an asylum seeker from Indonesia and describes this painting as an expression of what he saw and how he felt while being tortured.

**Stone Forest by Jiang Tie-Feng, floral artist Barbara Foss**
The original *Stone Forest* was commissioned by the People's Republic of China in 1979 as an 8'6" x 22'6" mural and hangs permanently in the Great Hall of the People, Tiananmen Square, Beijing. Jiang immigrated to the United States in 1983, eventually moved to Minnesota, and created this fine enhanced serigraph reproduction.

**Resilience by Kurt Seaberg, floral artist Therese Sexe**
This lithograph, by a Sami American, depicts the devastation of our environment along with a robin tending her nest to show the resilience of nature. Unity purchased this piece from his Parish Hall art show.

**Birches by Alice Hugy, floral artist Diane Grasse**
Alice Hugy was featured in the *In Her Own Right: Minnesota's First Generation of Women Artists* show at the Minnesota Museum of American Art (2007), and in the subsequent book *Pioneer Modernists: Minnesota's First Generation of Women Artists.* Birches was painted in 1970, a year before the Swiss-born artist passed away at age ninety-five.

***Integrity, Service & Joy*** **by Diane von Arx, floral artist Marty Rossman**
Unity commissioned the artist to learn about the church and create an original
work in 2016-17. She was among the calligraphers that created the internation-
ally known, handwritten St. John's Bible.

*Call to Worship*
**Down to the River to Pray**
**Rev. Karen Hering**

I grew up in a river town where, in my troubled teenage years, I sometimes went down to the river to pray. There, on the overgrown riverbank path bordering a Catholic cemetery, I walked past the Stations of the Cross: fourteen stone shrines, earlier abandoned, and some quite badly vandalized.

Not knowing the pilgrimage of prayer many Catholics make while visiting the stations, I would pause silently at each one, sitting on the bench across the path, gazing into the arched and empty stone shelters where an ancient story had once been told. Some shrines were strewn with sticks and leaves and mud; others were marred by paint and ugly words. A few still held the broken fragments of statues that had traced Jesus's tortured march through Jerusalem to his crucifixion.

I knew the story well, and often brought my journal to write my own words and stories; and on that riverbank, where ancient sorrows met those of my own heart and times, I was grateful to find a quiet peace.

Last fall, many of us went prayerfully down to the river here in St. Paul. Visiting sacred sites on the riverbanks not far from here, we learned the Dakota creation stories that locate the beginning of all life right there where the Minnesota and Mississippi Rivers meet, a sacred place the Dakota people call B'dote. B'dote, a place of birth, life, creation, and genesis. Almost one hundred of us from Unity have now attended a Sacred Sites Tour to learn the history of our riverbanks—stories of creation, birth, and genesis AND stories of the Dakota people's own tortured walk in 1862 from Mankato to the river valley here, where women, children, and elders were held by US forces in a concentration camp, and where several hundred died in the winter of 1863.

What does it mean to go down to the river to pray, when the muddy riverbanks hold footprints not only of birth, life, creation, and genesis, but also the footprints of imprisonment, suffering, and death?

Today, we gather for worship just a little downriver from B'dote, on Dakota land taken by white settlers long ago. We come together here in this sanctuary—and online—grateful for our slow return to in-person worship, grieving that it is still not complete, longing for the sense of home we knew before in this sacred place, and acknowledging that we have all been deeply changed by what we've lived through and what we've learned in the eighteen months gone by.

Today, in our cherished Merging of the Waters ceremony, let us remember the sacred ground of being that draws us together as a people of faith. Let us heed our call to unity—our unity with one another and with all people and all beings. Let us recognize the footprints made by us and others, today and in years gone by, in the muddy riverbanks we call home. This is how we'll find a path toward peace. This is how worship calls us all *into* the waters of birth, life, creation, and genesis.

Come, let us worship together.

*Note: The service, "Down to the River to Pray," in which this Call to Worship was delivered, was livestreamed on Sunday, September 12, 2021, at 9:00 a.m. To view the service, visit the Unity Church-Unitarian channel on YouTube, select the "Sunday Service" Playlist, and scroll down to find the date and title: www.youtube.com/c/unitychurchunitarian*

Waves
Amanda Reuter

***From the Pulpit***
**The Sing-Along**
**Rev. Shay MacKay**

After finishing my internship at Unity Church-Unitarian, I spent a year working as a chaplain in a senior living facility that included independent living, a nursing home, and memory care. One of the residents of the nursing home, Harriet, was an older woman with advanced dementia. She was mostly nonverbal and confined to a wheelchair, so the nurses would often bring her to sit in the common area to observe and be a part of whatever was happening that day.

During this time, Harriet would begin calling out, "Help me! Help me, please!" She would repeat this over and over, getting louder with each repetition. These were the only words we had ever heard her say, and no matter what any of us did, we could never find a reason (or solution) for her pleas— so we began to ignore them.

One day I was playing piano for the residents and Harriet kept calling out. At first, I played louder, then more gently, trying to find something that would soothe her into quiet so the other residents could listen to the music, but nothing worked.

I finally decided to see if this time anything was actually wrong, so I knelt in front of her wheelchair and took her hands in mine. I asked her what was wrong, and to my surprise, she answered, "Nothing is wrong."

I then asked her why she kept calling out for help and she looked directly in my eyes and said, "I don't need help, I was just singing along to the beautiful music."

*Note: This was delivered during the service, "The Story We Find Ourselves In," on Sunday, September 26, 2021, at 9:00 a.m. To view the service, visit the Unity Church-Unitarian channel on YouTube, select the "Sunday Service" Playlist, and scroll down to find the date and title: www.youtube.com/c/unitychurchunitarian*

## Practicing Resurrection
### Rev. Shay MacKay

I have, at times in my life, struggled with depression. During those times I always turn to music—both creating it and listening to it. There are songs that have held me as I've wept, songs that have renewed hope, songs that have helped me find life again.

Many years ago, during a particularly rough time, I was living in a place where I didn't have a piano. Fortunately, a friend of mine was able to somehow get me a key to a Catholic church she attended, and they had a baby grand piano I could play.

So, I would go, late at night, slip in through the shadows, into the silent sanctuary.

I would leave the lights off and remove my shoes, light a few candles in prayer, and then sit down and pour my heart out—playing whatever came, whatever needed to be said, whatever needed to be heard.

There I would sit, barefoot in the dark, weeping as I found life again through music in that still, sacred space—

Practicing resurrection with every note I played.

Who Are You?                                                    Kathy Schur

## Searching for Andromeda
## Cynthia Orange

We lie on a sleeping bag in an open field,
looking for Andromeda.

*"Focus on the fire over there, and then raise your eyes.*
*Find the North Star..."*

You know the stars by name and can explain why they
seem to race across the sky.

I search for the smudge that is another galaxy,
the thumbprint that does not belong to ours.

*"Find the 'W' of stars..."*

You chart my course, and I obediently follow with my eyes.

An occasional meteor escapes from space and is pulled
toward earth.

Why am I so drawn to Andromeda,
those distant stars that don't belong?

Other stars shoot across me while I dance alone.
I balance on the edge,
wishing that someone would chart their course by my fire.

Yellow Profusion                                                    Kathy Schur

## All the Way: Celebrating During a Pandemic
**Linny Mae Siems**

May 7, 2020: the 50th anniversary of when Bill E. and I met and began our life together. The traditional theme for a 50th anniversary is gold. I knew in my heart we needed to celebrate in a big way. The planning began that year in January!

First, the venue: I called Unity Church to book the Parish Hall. Next, music: I called Bill E's former bandmates to make sure they would save the date. Then, a myriad of details were addressed: a caterer chosen, guest list created, and invitations sent. Our girls and I shopped, and each of us bought a gold dress for the occasion! Every person I spoke with was willing to bend over backwards to help the cause.

Then, by mid-March, the Covid-19 pandemic shut down most everything. No one thought to be too concerned; all would be well by May. The party date, however, became impossible to keep; we were all still in lock-down isolation. We postponed until late summer, but that new date was postponed as well. Finally, with no end to the pandemic in sight, Unity Church suggested that we not reschedule until there was a clear sense of when the church would re-open, though when it did, we would be given top priority. There was no wiggle room and no alternative action to take.

We would not be celebrating our 50th as planned, and since Bill E. was living in a Long-Term Care (LTC) facility, quite possibly not even with each other. Eight years after being diagnosed with Parkinson's, Bill E. needed more care than I could give him at home and moved into Episcopal Church Home.

Determined to let Bill E. know of my on-going love for him and to honor this big milestone for us anyway, I put all my energy into a new plan. Our day would be made special in every way possible. With a new timeline and to do list, I barely slept, worried about not getting everything done in time. I wisely made an anniversary card for Bill E. and thank you cards for the staff the night before.

On May 7, 2021, I organized my errands so that I would have everything in place at Bill E.'s LTC in time for his lunch:

1. Cookies. I picked up four dozen cookies that I had ordered from our local bakery: ginger (Bill E.'s favorite!) and chocolate chip. These I would pass out to all the staff working day, evening, and night shifts; the other elders on his floor; the people at the front desk; the administration folks; and our family. The bakery gave me several smaller cookie bags to ease separating the correct number for each destination.
2. Flowers. The phone directions for picking up the huge bouquet of yellow flowers that I had ordered for Bill E.'s dining room table said to come to the back of the floral shop. I arrived for my scheduled

pickup, and I waited for an uncomfortable amount of time. Finally, I called to find out if everything was ok. They had been waiting for me out front, where there is a big sign that says: Pick Up Area.

3. Lunch. It was imperative to me that Bill E. and I have the identical lunch. Both of us grew up watching "Lunch with Casey," a local kids' TV show in the 50s and 60s featuring railroad conductor Casey Jones; we had loved the experience of eating the same lunch he was having.

After errands, I went home to deal with how the world operated during Covid. At the LTC, no one was allowed in the building.

Each item to be delivered to Bill E.'s LTC had to be in its own paper bag with every detail marked and labeled: where it was going, who it was going to, and who it was from. I was required to put on gloves and count out the number of cookies that went to each area and put them in the separate cookie bags. I sorted out which cards went into which bags. I put his lunch in a separate bag. I used a special vase for the floral bouquet and found a box to keep it safe in transport.

I made the deadline for his lunch time. It took several trips from my car. I had to leave everything on a table in the foyer, to be delivered by staff when they were available. It took an incredible amount of faith and trust in the staff on my part to leave these precious items and walk away.

The next challenge was to find a way to communicate with him in person. I asked the social worker to bring him to his window on the 4th floor so, with me in the parking lot, we could see each other, but she was in care conferences and couldn't. I asked the Activities Director and her assistant, but they were leading groups. I asked the Nurse Manager; she was not available.

Yet, one of these women heard the plea in my voice, had compassion, and found a random person to be Bill E.'s helper. To this day, I don't know either who it was that found help or who the help turned out to be. At long last, Bill E. was wheeled to his window—the tall, oversized kind that only opens four inches from the bottom (for safety reasons).

I waved up to him and shouted, "Happy anniversary!"

His helper bent down to get her mouth by the low opening and shouted back to me, "He says happy anniversary to you, too."

I yelled up to him, "I love you!"

The helper yelled back to me, "He says he loves you, too."

By then, I was laughing and crying, seeing this scene as it must look to an observer, like in a movie. I turned around and hugged myself so he could see my back with hands caressing me. There was nothing more to say or do. I walked to my car and went home.

Throughout that day, I was touched by the thoughtfulness, kindness, and generosity of our friends. Waiting for me on our back patio was a lovely card, a bouquet of homegrown flowers, and chocolates. Later, I answered the doorbell to dear friends bringing a lovely bouquet of flowers and a homemade card. Once again, the doorbell rang and more good buddies stood there with more flowers, a card, and expressions on their faces that brought me to tears. I received phone calls and cards in the mail as well. How could this be happening? So much goodness.

Our daughter, Willie, wanted to be a part of celebrating with me. There was no question that I wanted and needed to be with her. She brought dinner and desert, and we bundled up and sat on the back patio (another Covid determiner). Through tears and laughter and amazement, it felt so good to share my day.

Before it got dark, a car came down the alley and stopped in our driveway. Two dear friends came through our gate, each carrying a big black case. The woman opened up her case and brought out chilled champagne and four glasses. We toasted to fifty years, to what love looks like, and to friendship.

Then the man opened up his guitar case, and asked permission to sing his chosen song for the evening, "All the Way." And would I care to join him by whistling part of the song? Everything in me said: YES! At that moment, the power of the music felt big enough to carry all that would pour out of me in response to life's unfolding mystery.

I did not want this day to end. The disappointment of no big, gold party and the dread of being without Bill E. at my side to celebrate was lifted from my heart. I shared with Willie my utter astonishment at how the day evolved. She said, "I'm a bit like you, Mama. I like recognition. I told your friends that if they found it in their hearts to reach out to you in some way today, to please do so. And look what happened!"

Fifty years ago, Bill E. and I each found the person who could balance us. "To fall in love was to be caught, to be saved," as Kate Morton wrote.

I called Bill E. the day after our 50th and said, "Happy one day after our anniversary."

He replied, "It feels like a lot of planets have gone by."

*Note: I would like to offer my deepest gratitude to the loving spirits of our beloved community who stepped forward for us to honor our commitment, our efforts at doing the hard work of relationship, and to witness our rite of passage. Even social distancing from six feet away.*

**Allure**
**Bill E. Webb**

My beloved has caught my eye once again,
Calling me back to another time and place in our lives.
Her image raises my brow as she walks forever,
Silhouetted against the gray matter in my head,
Her picture is tucked safely away in a warm woolen sock,
The one that holds the most delicate and savored memories,

Still bearing the impression set by my heart so many years ago.
In an early morning ritual she leaves for work,
Going across the yard,
Unaware that she shines like a beacon.
Her movements energize the surrounding air,
And the morning begins to dance with the sun.
I am behind her, strung on a ladder peering through the steps,
Hoping she knows that I am looking for her throughout the day.

This memory answers a prayer that seeks rejuvenation,
A remembrance and witness to love's reaching act.
It floods my heart,
And I succumb to the rushing waters that deepen my sense of the holy,
Filling spaces that become revived through this touch of her presence.

After so many years of growth and change, ours is a tangled mess of
Life's feelings, fussing, fighting and freedom.
We are who we are, stretching and pulling, still shining together,
Much like the soul as it travels about in life's bends and turns,
Reflecting the light of God.

I wish to challenge myself and avoid complacency,
I struggle to understand this driving movement,
The one that keeps me trying to be the "one" with my beloved.

At times the light grows dim, and I become afraid,
Knowing that life offers up many twists, turns and opportunities.
Some are required tests with answers that clearly should not be pursued,
The impulse to change away from the light is often short-lived,

There are, and will continue to be,
Moments that affect us both individually and as a couple.
Sharing those times helps to shift the load once again,
As we hike along,
Sometimes dry with thirst for other things,
Or drenched with the awareness of life's abundant gifts.

When I am reacquainted with an instance of my own life's light and love,
I then consider that truth indeed means one needs faith,

And faith is often expressed through knowing that more love remains to be
found in the days ahead,
Especially when the faith has been sustained
by drawing from the well of the past.

The light that shone in the yard so many years ago,
Still lights the path that i am on today.
When I stop to re-think certain moments in my heart's journey,
I surprise myself with those memories drawn from the sock.

The jagged, coarse stone that years ago started out
To be caressed by the loving waters and sun,
Has become smooth over time.
Does the prospect of becoming a speck of sand frighten me?
What am I in this evolution?
Can I see where I am in this journey?

Am I the driftwood wanderer who floats along?
Or, am I the stone that stays put year after year?
My growing ability to perceive the movement of the stone,
Has me wondering.

—*March 16, 2001*

Black and Red Broadbill
Caroline Foster

**Chair**
**Gary Mabbott**

Walking home from the bakery,
I came upon an old chair in the alleyway.
Its rich red leather upholstery,
once worthy of a banker's office,
now looked chafed and tattered.

It had been the type of chair
in which an eighteen-year-old boy
might be made to wait,
in his rented tuxedo,
for a young lady
adorned in taffeta and curls
whom he would barely recognize.
It was a sturdy piece of furniture
with husky armrests shaped like
rolled rugs, and a high back
to lean the day's troubles against.

It must have been a good place
to sit and sip a cup of coffee
or a glass of wine,
watching the snow fall,
listening to Paul Simon,
or to take a nap,
like sitting in first-class,
head back, the inertia of lift-off
pressing you down.

Cats, too, would nap here
in the afternoon sun,
curled peacefully on the soft cushion,
whereas teenagers preferred
their spine against one armrest
with legs dangling over the other
as Michelangelo imagined
Jesus in his Pieta.

In its time the chair watched
dozens of movies
and swallowed pounds of popcorn,
coins and car keys,
as well as embraced feverish children
wrapped in blankets.
It was always home at Thanksgiving
and sat in the center
of each family photo.
Such was its steadfastness.

The aroma from my warm bread
reminded me of my own duty.
So, I tipped my hat to the chair
to acknowledge its devotion
and departed.

## Sleep
**Gary Mabbott**

Late at night, when he goes to bed
browsing a book or poem
he sings the fireflies to sleep
and bids the muses roam
the land of imagination
to fetch their stories home.

On the back of his eyelids
they paint hallucinations,
of flying around the house,
talking to vegetation,
and other eerie things
inviting interpretation,

of feeling lost, at great cost,
in melting railroad stations,
missing meetings with his boss
and Russian delegations,
or standing naked in front
of well-dressed congregations.

Sometimes, he gets out of bed,
often he needs to pee.
Mostly, his body goes along,
at times his mind walks free.
Normally, he scorns the light,
now and then he bangs his knee.

After the theater closes,
when all the drama's gone,
housekeeping springs into action,
the night shift carries on.
The physical plant is made ready
for the coming dawn.

The head custodian clears out
the rubble of the day:
whose home run beat the White Sox?
how many miles to Taipei?
casual conversations and
things he forgot to say.
Some pictures prove worth keeping;
a few facts should be retained.
Pathways between pixels should
be mended and maintained.
Models, motions, and meanings
must be filed and sustained.

Tak means yes in Polish;
Dziekuje means thank you.
His niece resembles Grandma;
E equals h times Nu.
B diminished resolves to C;
viruses cause the flu.

Ultimately this jumble
becomes organized instead.
When the morning breaks and
he finally gets out of bed,
why should he feel rested,
after such hubbub in his head?

Tree Shadows                                              Amanda Reuter

# Pomegranate, Kale, Wild Rice Salad

**Salad:**
- 1 cup pomegranate seeds
- 2 cups chopped Kale
- 1/4 cup toasted walnuts
- 4-5 sliced green onions
- 1 cup cooked wild rice
- 1/4 cup feta cheese

**Dressing:**
- 3 tablespoons olive oil
- 1 tablespoon red wine vinegar
- 1 tablespoon honey
- 1/2 teaspoon salt

Toss the salad ingredients together. Mix the dressing ingredients well and combine with the salad.

Lisa Burke

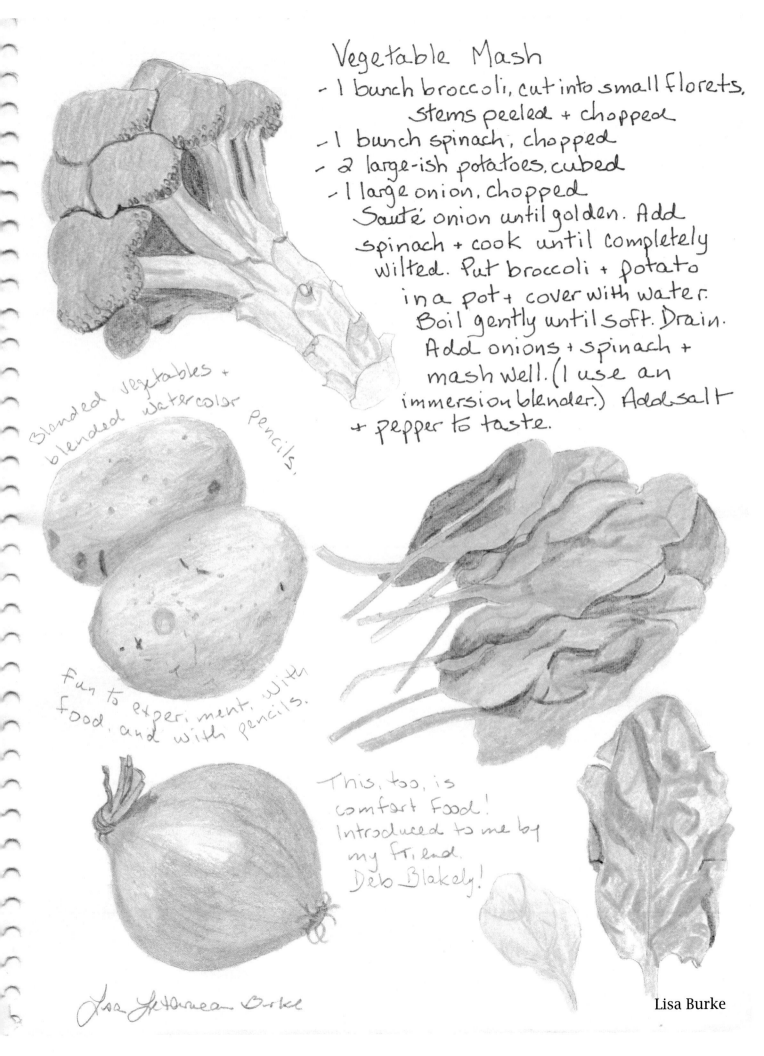

# Vegetable Mash

- 1 bunch broccoli, cut into small florets, stems peeled + chopped
- 1 bunch spinach, chopped
- 2 large-ish potatoes, cubed
- 1 large onion, chopped

Sauté onion until golden. Add spinach + cook until completely wilted. Put broccoli + potato in a pot + cover with water. Boil gently until soft. Drain. Add onions + spinach + mash well. (I use an immersion blender.) Add salt + pepper to taste.

Blended vegetables + blended watercolor pencils.

Fun to experiment with food, and with pencils.

This, too, is comfort food! Introduced to me by my friend, Deb Blakely!

Lisa Burke

## Jess and the Little Boy
## Shelley Butler

The little boy sat on the big easy chair by the big picture window, both made all the larger by his size, which to Jess seemed to be small for a five-year old. Jess knew of course, but asked anyway, "What's your name? How old are you?"

He turned away from gazing out the window to look at her as if he had not known she was there. After considering her for a second or two, he turned back to the window.

Trying another tactic, she asked, "Are you hungry? We have fresh blueberry muffins, just made this morning," as if there was a "we" and not just an "I."

Jess wasn't sure if she detected a smile or if that was wishful thinking, but the little boy scooched himself off the chair and made his way to the table, where he sat down, helped himself to a napkin and a muffin, and began peeling the paper cup off of the muffin. Jess poured him a glass of milk and set it down next to his plate. He picked it up and drank from it as if no one had thought to give him a drink for a long time.

"OK, so that's how it's going to be," Jess said. "That's fine. I'm used to a quiet house, and if you don't want to talk to me, you don't have to, little boy."

As soon as she said it, she regretted calling him a "little boy," remembering that the worst thing people said to her was that she was a "little" anything: "girl, gal, sprite, chickadee, rascal." She would have to start thinking of and calling him by his name, but Samuel Ethan Jorgensen II was such a big name for this small of a person.

"I guess we're alike in that I'm a person of few words, too," she said. "But tell me one thing: do you go by Sam?"

He shook his head in disgust.

"When your Grandpa dropped you off, he called you 'Buddy.' Should I call you 'Buddy,' too?"

He cocked his head to the side as if puzzling on the question and gave enough of a nod in her direction to indicate approval. If that didn't look familiar, Jess didn't know what did. Her parents had always told her not to do that, it being disrespectful. But if anything, it made Jess feel the glimmer of a connection to the little boy, to Buddy.

Jess had never known Buddy before, not really, even though she had carried him for eight months. As soon as she told Sam that she was pregnant, and yes, he was the father, Sam went home and told his parents the awful news: that he'd never loved her but just hooked up with her one night (which wasn't true). Sam's parents stepped in and took over, as they were wont to do with any adversity that had come before Sam.

Her parents were gone, she was alone in the little cabin she had inherited on Lake Superior, and even if Sam wanted to step up to father the baby (which he didn't), he was shipping out for basic training in three weeks. She took the deal: she would carry the baby to term, taking excellent care of her health, and the Jorgensons would pay for everything, provided that she give over the baby upon birth and never see them, the baby, or Sam ever again.

The baby was born four weeks early at just under six pounds, for which the Jorgensons blamed her. Her punishment was not to be allowed to hold the baby because he was too delicate to be passed around. Not long after, they took the baby and moved some 560 miles away to Mitchell, SD, near the world's only structure made completely out of corn. She hadn't heard from them since the hospital, until Earl called yesterday to say he was giving the boy back.

"What should we do now?" Jess asked Buddy.

Was he looking at her like she was clueless? He picked up his bag and pointed to a partially open door.

"Yes, that's your room," Jess confirmed. She watched in awe as he gathered his courage and crossed the threshold into a new life. She heard a zipper opening and then closing, drawers opening and then closing, a creak of the bed, what maybe was pages of a book turning, a chuckle here and there, followed by a long sigh, and finally the sound of regular breathing.

"He's unpacked, read himself a story, and put himself to bed," Jess marveled. Now it made sense why he was dressed in short pants, a dress shirt with a clip-on bow tie, and a jacket to match—he was as much a little man as his clothes were a little man's suit.

* * *

"WHO ARE YOU?"

Jess's eyes snapped open as jackrabbit fast as if someone had stuck her with a hot poker. What the... Oh yeah, Buddy.

"Good morning," she said, eyeing him with some clarity now. "And why are you yelling?"

"I didn't yell the first three times I tried to wake you up. I even pulled the covers off you, but it was like you was dead. Who are you?" Buddy asked again.

Jess looked down and saw that indeed the sheet had been pulled down to the end of the bed.

"Do you want some breakfast?" she asked.

"Nah, I already ate. Who are you?" he persisted.

"You ate? What did you eat?"

"Muffin, peanut butter, banana, and milk. Who are you?"

"You put peanut butter on a blueberry muffin?"

"No," he said impatiently, "I ate it with a spoon. WHO ARE..."

"OK, OK," Jess said, unable to dodge the question any longer. "Can I get some coffee first?"

"I brought you some," Buddy said, pointing to the cup on the side table.

Jess took a big swig without thinking and fought the almost uncontrollable urge to gag. "You know how to use the microwave, I see," she said. "You found coffee in the pot from yesterday?"

"Sure. Mama never wasted anything and always drank the leftovers," he explained. "Why? Don't you like it?"

While she was deciding how not to hurt his feelings, she did a double take.

"Mama?" Jess asked. "You have a Mama?"

"Not anymore," Buddy said matter-of-factly. "She died. My brother Sam died, too."

"I'm so sorry," Jess murmured, figuring out that "Mama" was really grandma and "my brother Sam" was really his father. "That must have been very hard for you."

"I see dead people. They're everywhere." Buddy said, mimicking the kid in *The Sixth Sense.* "That's from Sam's favorite movie. He let me watch it with him when Mama wasn't around. 'I see dead people. They're everywhere.' We used to say that all the time and never told Mama. It was our secret."

Jess took another swig of coffee, as disgusting as it was, feeling the need to wake up even more, if only to be sure she was hearing what she was hearing.

"If it was a secret, why are you telling me?"

"They're both dead. I see dead people..."

"OK, OK," Jess interrupted. She pointed to her jeans on the floor and then to the door. Following her finger down then up, Buddy got it and went out to let her get dressed.

Buddy was again sitting in the big easy chair by the window when she came out—*her* big easy chair by the window. She'd have to do something about that. Maybe get a second chair or something, maybe learn to like the couch. But she was relieved to see he was wearing something other than the suit, even if it was stainless and perfectly creased khakis.

"Soooo," Jess began, not really sure where to begin. "Who did Grandpa tell you that I was?"

"Just a lady who could take care of me better than he could. He didn't talk much." He looked at her like that again, puzzling on something and cocking his head. "Mmm... I don't know if he was right though. I had to make my own breakfast this morning."

"If you can make your own breakfast, why shouldn't you make your own breakfast?" Jess asked.

"I'm five, remember?" He cocked his head and asked, "Did you know I was five?"

I am completely out of my league, Jess thought as she nodded.

"Hey, who are you anyway?" Buddy asked yet again.

"Hmmm...," Jess stalled. She walked over to the bookcase as if she was looking for something there, as if she might find a way out in one of her books. Not finding anything there, she turned around suddenly.

"Hey, do you like puppies? Let's go get a puppy!" Jess said impulsively.

Buddy leaped off the chair and ran to the door with the energy of a thoroughbred racehorse, grabbing her hand on the way, and off they went to get a puppy, wherever the hell they could do that.

"I'll have to figure that out on the way," Jess thought as they got in the car, "as well as what to say the next time he asks." She turned left onto Highway 61, heading southeast toward Duluth—a boy and his mother-that-he-didn't-know-was-his mother looking for a life raft.

*Note: This story is part of a larger work of fiction in progress entitled "Just Jess."*

The Last Leaf                                                    Nancy Birger

**Our Next Presenter**
**Paul Englund**

Our next presenter
has been writing poems on and off
since 8th grade, or was it 10th?

Well anyway
around 50 years
and pretty much
unnoticed.

In his hometown of
South St. Paul, Minnesota,
he is not considered
a living cultural icon,
nor is his birthplace
down the road in West St. Paul
a destination of literary pilgrims.

His work has not been hailed as
"luminous"
in the New York Times.

It surprised no one in 2017
when he was not a close contender for the
Walt Whitman Award
and consequently
the committee did not have to regret
that their by-laws
would not permit them
to split the honors into two awards of $2,500
each.

His most recent body of work
"Poems of Old Age"
will not be published later this year by
Farrar, Straus & Giroux;
predictably
there will be no pre-publication praise
on the dust jacket
from
well-known writers

(including Billy Collins
who will make no
droll observations
concerning the author's unique voice).

Finally
although he is clearly not a writer who
needs no introduction
I would simply note that
he has never been described as the
Poet Laureate
of his generation
and his work
hasn't
touched the hearts
of so many.

*Cairns Editors' Note: But his work has clearly touched our hearts!*

## When Jesus Comes Back
## Paul Englund

When Jesus comes back
Then it will be settled
Once and for all.

It'll be on the news
And even the scientists
Will have to believe it.

Then those of us who doubted
Will be embarrassed
And not know exactly
What to do.

And those who were sure—
Absolutely Sure—
(If such there be)
They can be happy
Because they were right all along
And that always feels good.

Window into the Soul                                          Molly Rodich

**Drawing the Circle Wider**
**Barbara Foss**

It's surely a bit of a cliché to limit recollections to where we were and what we were doing at the moment we encountered the shocking news that a sudden onslaught of airplanes was commandeered for destruction twenty years ago this past September. Almost everyone who was over the age of five in 2001 has a story. "I'll never forget..."

In my case, the impact of 9/11 is why my husband and I are now at Unity, although that was not in any way on our minds that sunny and dark September day.

As churches nationwide and around the world filled with shocked and emotionally paralyzed worshipers the Sundays immediately following 9/11, we, too, were seeking comfort and trying to make some sense of the world. We wedged into tight spaces in overflow seating packed with people we knew well or didn't know at all—the Christmas-Easter Crowd—hoping for clarity and reason.

Our sizable ELCA (Evangelical Lutheran Church of America) congregation in a large, mostly white, and Christian-identifying southern suburb of the Twin Cities had been good to us. We'd been transferred to Minnesota in 1991, discovered this church and were drawn in by the strong outreach ministry and focus on music and education. The spiritual leaders were solid and supportive, and the familiar hymns and liturgical seasons made us feel at home in our new community.

For over a decade it was comfortable and enriching to be part of this religious family. From here, my husband Pat co-led multiple youth and adult Habitat for Humanity and other rebuild-type mission trips into inner-city Milwaukee, up to the flooded Red River Fargo region, and around the Twin Cities. I was fortunate to join this church's marvelously gifted choir; its professional direction and talent eventually led to a collaborative performance at Carnegie Hall with the Augsburg College Choir. We were warmly held by this generous, friendly Lutheran body which comforted us through the decline of three of our parents. Our spirituality felt alive.

But something weird happened...

Months after 9/11, we started to sense a them-versus-us environment. Our pastoral staff—five strong—were showing some dissonance. Two of them were eager to learn more about world religions, and reached out to neighbors who didn't look like us or worship as we did. They even advocated for ethnic foods at church potlucks, along with the lime Jell-O and Tater Tot casseroles.

The other three ministers seemed to lean toward defending America's uniqueness as entitled land, spackling any cracks in the safe wall around us.

Regularly, they affirmed this by closing worship with the hymn "America the Beautiful."

> Oh, beautiful for patriot dream
> That sees beyond the years
> Thine alabaster cities gleam,
> Undimmed by human tears!
> America! America!
> God shed his grace on thee,
> And crown thy good with brotherhood
> From sea to shining sea.

My husband and I discovered—somewhat to our surprise, he being an Air Force Veteran—that we were not the flag-flying, red-white-and-blue patriots that seemed, to us, to be finding comfort in a kind of defensive arrogance. We were even, perhaps, embarrassed for our country's growing self-righteousness. A familiar caution echoed from my mother's sage advice: Was our country becoming "holier than thou"?

We were confused. Why were American citizens with valid fears of, and understandable hostility toward, the 9/11 terrorists channeling their emotions into distrusting anyone who spoke, dressed, ate, or worshipped differently than they did?

The poem "Outwitted," by Edwin Markham, began regularly floating through my mind:

> He drew a circle that shut me out—
> Heretic, rebel, a thing to flout.
> But love and I had the wit to win:
> We drew a circle and took him In!

I heard these words as a revelation. Who were we, as Americans, to generically call "others" our enemies? Were so many coping by drawing the circle smaller, shutting out those who were not like them? The circle was the promise!

A transition began for us that year. The church we'd loved would be fine without us, we decided. Perhaps we didn't really want to be part of any church again—mainline religions dropped off our radar.

We began to feel a draw to the city. We started thinking about moving from our spacious suburban home and yard to a smaller dwelling. Perhaps a condo with a lower environmental footprint, in a diverse urban neighborhood, near a farmers' market.

We were reading about world religions and feeling less sure that there is only one way to heaven; and maybe heaven isn't even the intended destination!

Dreaming big about going small seemed like an antidote to so much of what we were finding unsettling.

When the fifth anniversary of that horrific day came around, we had drastically downsized our acquisitions from over thirty-five years of marriage and parenting. We'd moved into the city near downtown St. Paul, to a condo in a diverse and walkable neighborhood, and were enthusiastically tuning into the issues of our newly adopted locale. Unlike the Starbucks which sparked many mornings in the suburbs, the nearby independent coffee shop was a microcosm of diversity with a "please share your table" philosophy, enhanced by a fascinating array of Minnesota winter costuming.

Here, we could be part of drawing the circle wider.

Our walks eventually took us past the corner of Grotto and Portland in St. Paul, and curiosity drew us in through the doors of Unity. We hadn't a clue what Unitarian Universalism was, but we were greeted, from day one, with inclusiveness, spectacular music, and the weirdness and relief of having no repetitive liturgy or creed. The readers, preachers, and musicians seemed to know our story, to be talking directly to us. And the real coffee was served in real cups with real cream.

But most of all, two of the first hymns we sang brought tears to our eyes and suggested we'd found the spiritual home we had been sure, five years earlier, we were *not* seeking.

The first was the rallying hymn "Draw the Circle Wide." There it was, that persistent phrase I'd heard running through my mind: "We drew a circle and took him In!" Joining a congregation of voices surrounding us at Unity we sang words of welcome, inclusivity, expansiveness, and generosity. "Draw the circle wide, draw it wider still." No one would be left standing by themselves.

The second hymn, "This is My Song, O God of All the Nations," was "America the Beautiful" taken to a higher, wider level. It was a prayer for peace across the globe and reaffirmed that everyone, everywhere had hopes and dreams. It underscored what I would soon learn was the first Unitarian principle, affirming the worth and dignity of all people: "A song of peace for their land and for mine."

9/11 changed me. It shocked me into a world far larger and greater than I'd ever experienced. It challenged my comfortable lifelong beliefs. It opened my ears and eyes to plights I'd never before acknowledged. It aimed me *away* from assuming easy comfort and *toward* the stark reality of inequity in society. It led me to Unity, where the questions and challenges are never easy, but the rewards are abundant.

Peterson Family Spiral                                    Beth Peterson

## When Curiosity Becomes Faith
Rebecca Gonzalez-Campoy

"It Starts With Faith," or so claims the "Organizing School for Teams" webinar that I completed this fall from the Side with Love public advocacy campaign of the Unitarian Universalist Association. That wasn't true for me when I began to determine my next right action following the murder of George Floyd in May 2020. "It all starts with curiosity… and a commitment to making a difference" comes closer to my origin story of social justice engagement.

A desire to learn more about bringing spirituality to antiracism work motivated me to enroll in the Master of Divinity program at United Theological Seminary of the Twin Cities (UTS) in September 2020, nearly four decades after earning a BA. Now, well into the second year, I'm pondering the addition of UU Studies to my Social Transformation track. Curiosity can be expensive and time-consuming, but the learning is so worthwhile.

I arrived at seminary with little religious baggage to unload, and limited exposure to sacred text. I also knew little about UU history except that our ancestors included major players in politics, literature, and education. I grew up in the 1960s and 1970s and UU religious education focused more on learning about other churches than on UU content. The Unitarians and Universalists had just finalized their merger—they were still sorting things out.

What a year of growth in knowledge, perspective, and, yes, spirituality! My classmates, mostly from progressive faiths, hail from all over the US and Canada, span a range of ages, and encompass a wide variety of racial, sexual, and gender identities. Their tough questions during discussions, calling it like it is, push us all to think more critically. We learned early on about "Ouch! Oops!" (naming hurtful remarks, acknowledging then apologizing for them). Sharing stories of deep pain and joyful resilience enriches each of us. Whether it's "Religious and Theological Interpretation" or "Queer and Trans Theologies," it doesn't matter. Our interactions with texts and each other bring us closer to understanding our own theology and how we plan to live our beliefs.

While UUs are in UTS leadership and instruction, we're still the heretics in the room. That became *really* evident during the "History of Christian Theologies" class where the Catholic and Reformation leaders kept killing off our UU ancestors or sending them into exile. At the same time, "UU History and Polity" (taught by former Unity minister Rev. Lisa Friedman) revealed that our ancestors landed on both sides of the national narrative—that of oppressors and of the oppressed. She introduced us to the many works of Rev. Mark Morrison-Reed, expert on UU Black history. Through essays and original documents, he demonstrated how Unitarians and Universalists alike rejected many opportunities to co-create our faith with Black Americans throughout our history. Yet they influenced and shaped who we are today. And they continue to do so.

So far, the biggest challenge to my education is myself. As a former journalist and a life-long UU (in practice, if not church attendance), I question. I have been trained to observe and report, rather than offer an interpretation; I'm used to leaving that up to my audience. My instructors' expectations are forcing me out of my comfort zone.

My MDiv journey and subsequent social justice volunteering at Unity is turning into my own Book of Revelations. And I give credit to Rev. Karen Hering for continuing to send me useful ideas and suggestions for every chapter. Joining a Wellspring Wednesday presentation by Rev. Jim Bear Jacobs in October 2020 led to my helping to start the Indigenous Justice Community Outreach Ministry Team at Unity. The commitment to Indigenous justice connected me to the Native American Boarding School Healing Coalition. Learning more about the horrific impact these schools had on Native American children and their families meant coming to the sobering realization that my parents' adoption of my brother from the White Earth Reservation in 1966 was nothing more than an extension of the US government's effort to destroy Native American families. I know my parents had no idea of this connection, but nonetheless, my brother's life did not go well living in a white household in a white society. Through a workshop offered by Twin Cities-based Antiracism Study Dialogue Circles, I learned about the Doctrine of Discovery and white colonization.

Once COVID-19 restrictions relaxed, I ventured out to Rev. Jacobs' Sacred Sites Tour, wandered around Four Sisters Farmers Market outside the All My Relations Art Gallery, took in the latest exhibit of Native American art inside, attended a local Pow Wow, all the while seeking ways to build relationships.

As I put my MDiv Social Transformation project together (think of this as a thesis plan), I incorporated helping to develop Unity's Justice Database, leading a Black Films Canon series, and helping to coordinate the Antiracism Literacy Partnership. This is where my "UU History and Polity" class comes in handy—you must know how an organization works to effectively contribute to what it does.

Every connection leads to more opportunities to learn, grow, and make a difference. Just when I think my eyes are at their widest, observations by others push me to consider not only what I see, but to also notice what I do NOT. Instead of being satisfied that finally women are in charge of the "good" team when watching *The Last Jedi* (the first assignment for "Art, Religion, and Contemporary Culture"), ask why are whites still in charge even in the future? Instead of privately wondering how marginalized people could possibly want to belong to a faith that has done nothing but oppress them, consider how they make that sacred text their own. And remember that what is mainstream for one group is not so for another.

I strive to listen deeply and hear the voices of others and of my inner self. When I do, I see the world more clearly. My curiosity is fully alive, but my heart is breaking open, too. Is that starting with faith? Yes, now it is.

Shades of Gray in Rocky Mountain National Park, Paul Rogne

## The Litany of Relinquishment:
## The Ministry of Rob and Janne Eller-Isaacs

During the worship service of May 16, 2021, the Unity Church congregation acknowledged the end of the ministry of Janne and Rob Eller-Isaacs and released them from service to the church through "The Litany of Relinquishment." The congregation was represented by Clover Earl, a current trustee, Ken Green, and Rebecca Flood.

Ken Green: It is an honor to represent the search team that proposed Janne and Rob Eller-Isaacs to become the ministerial candidates for Unity Church-Unitarian. After a year of search, on May 21, 2000, the members of Unity Church called Janne and Rob to serve as our Senior Co-Ministers. They were installed the following November. We who served on the "old" search team have every confidence that the new search team will select a candidate to service Unity Church in the years to come just as faithfully as have Janne and Rob Eller-Isaacs.

Rebecca Flood: As a trustee, I represented the board in the act of installation. Almost twenty-one years ago, I spoke these words as part of the act of installation. Will you join with me in reading responsively?

>    For this church and its ministry in this place, for its teachings, and the faith that sustains us:

>    Congregation: We Give Thanks.

>    Rebecca: For those who came before us, who worshipped here and whose memory still lights the path we walk together:

>    Congregation: We Give Thanks.

Rebecca: Rob and Janne, we promised to walk together in the unity of the spirit and in the bond of peace. Together, we have responded to the demands of justice. We have created a fruitful and nourishing shared ministry that lives out in every facet of congregational life. Your ministry has blessed us in private moments as well as public. You have reminded us to keep expanding our sense of welcome. You have been with us in our greatest hours of need and in our times of triumph. You have faithfully witnessed as we crossed important thresholds in our lives.

Congregation: We Give Thanks.

Janne and Rob Eller-Isaacs: We thank the members and friends of Unity Church for walking this path with us. We are grateful for all that we have learned from you. We thank you for the love, kindness, and support you have shown us. We ask that you forgive us for our mistakes, for unintended slights, for ways that we have disappointed or missed the mark. We are grateful for the ways that our vision and leadership has been embraced and shared. It is right that we leave now to make room for other styles of leadership. Your future is bright and promising. We leave with confidence in your ministry. As we leave, we carry all that we have learned and the many gifts we have received from being in relationship with you and your families.

Congregation: We welcome your gratitude, offer our forgiveness, and know that it is right for you to end your ministry here. We will not forget all that we have learned from you. We thank you for your time among us. We ask your forgiveness for our mistakes and ways we disappointed you. Your influence on our faith and our efforts in living lives of integrity, service, and joy will not end at your departure.

Janne and Rob: We forgive you and accept your gratitude. May this moment mark the completion of our active service among you. We celebrate the opportunity our retirement presents to you to embrace new leadership. Our shared ministry has been a blessing and we hope has served a larger love and our deepening faith.

Clover Earl: Do you, the members and friends of Unity Church, release Janne and Rob from the duties of Senior Co-Ministers?

Congregation: We do. We offer our encouragement for their ministry as it unfolds in new ways.

Clover Earl: Do you, Janne and Rob, release the congregation from turning to you and depending on you?

Janne and Rob: We do.

Clover: Do you offer your encouragement for the continued ministry here and the relationship with another who will come to serve? Will you pledge to covenant with your successor so that their ministry is fully embraced and supported?

Janne and Rob: We do, and we will.

Clover: On behalf of the members and friends of Unity Church, I am witness to the words spoken: words of gratitude, forgiveness, and release. We pledge our support in the transitions signified in this service.

Rev. Karen Hering: And will you pray with us. Holy one, who holds the times and seasons, we give thanks for the lineage of love and leadership that has brought us this day, and for the growth and grace that our years with Rob and Janne have brought us... May we each and all be as blessed in this parting as we have been by our time together.

*Note: The litany was read responsively during the service, "From Holding On and Letting Go," which was livestreamed on Sunday, May 16, 2021, 10:00 a.m. To view the service, visit the Unity Church-Unitarian channel on YouTube, select the "Sunday Service" Playlist, and scroll down to find the date and title: www.youtube.com/c/unity-churchunitarian*

Spellbound                                            Peggy Wright

*From the Pulpit*
**Lost**
**Rev. Kathy Hurt**

Fledgling ministers are required, during the years it takes to earn final fellowship (the professional credentials our denomination mandates for those who want to serve our congregations), to have a mentor and to meet with that mentor regularly. This seems a wise expectation, given the significant learning curve a new minister faces as they leave the safety of the seminary and head out into the wild world of actual congregations. When I completed seminary studies and started with my first congregation, out in Minnesota Valley, I headed off to the initial meeting with my mentor quite convinced that I had nothing else to learn. After all, my ministerial internship here at Unity had gone quite well; I had graduated seminary with honors; I was a smart cookie; so, what else did I need to do ministry well?

My mentor surprised me by not addressing all those skills I already had, but by throwing me into a crucial learning ministers need to serve congregations, namely the world of perceptions. "A minister," he said, "is a walking Rorschach blot. As such, you will be the target of your congregation's projections. And this goes both ways, for your congregation will be a Rorschach blot for you. Both of you trigger projections onto one another."

You and I are in the first stage of our interim journey together. We bring to this journey myriad expectations, wondering whether each will live up to the reputation that has preceded us (perhaps fearing the other will live up to the reputation that has preceded us); and with myriad anxieties, wondering just how this is going to work, whether it will work at all, whether we will find this year a measure of satisfaction and growth along with the predictable challenges, or just one challenge after another. Expectations and anxieties on both sides are laced with projections that can make it difficult to distinguish the reality from the perception, the minister and the congregation from the Rorschach blot. While you and I have the benefit of not being complete strangers to one another, still, Rorschach blots are devilishly difficult to decipher. How can you know whether you see the person or the projection, the Rorschach and the reality? Am I seeing you as the congregation you are today? Are you seeing me as nothing more than a minister who is not Rob and Janne? For in order to do good ministry together, it seems crucial that we be able to see just who it is we are dealing with.

We continue this morning our worship theme of vocation, a theme that may sound utterly misplaced where a transitional year with an interim minister is concerned. All those descriptions—transitional, interim—suggest not the clarity and purpose of a vocation, but the absence of vocation. A transition means there is no calling, right? "Interim time" is by definition a between time, a time of waiting for vocation, right? Many congregations associate interim ministry and a ministerial transition with the word *lost*: lost time, lost energy, lost focus. Perhaps being lost is exactly the point. In the vocation of an interim year, congregations go through an interim to get lost, to lose themselves, because being lost is a significant spiritual experience; not an experience we want but an experience that we seem to need.

"I once was lost, but now I'm found." We sing those words, often with some emotion, in that traditional familiar hymn, "Amazing Grace." Composed by John Newton after an experience of nearly being lost in a storm at sea, and after a lifetime of being lost in a series of bad business ventures and unhappy relationships, the hymn celebrates the wonder of being found, how sweet it is to be found when being lost was all there was.

"I once was lost, but now I'm found." I have been lost more times than I care to remember, so "Amazing Grace" inspires in me a special gratitude for being found. Sometimes I have been minimally lost and only for a short time, as I have been in my relocation from Louisville and an interim ministry there to Saint Paul and Unity. I wade through my lostness learning names and places as quickly and gracefully as possible, eager to be done with the time of not knowing anything.

Other times my lostness has been deeper and more painful, as when I was lost following the ending of primary relationships or lost following my exit from my childhood religious traditions and all the comfort and familiarity they brought. Sometimes I have been lost so thoroughly and for such a long time that I began to fear I would be lost forever: I have been lost in my life when I could not find a ministry that called to me; I have been lost in my heart when I fell into the dark space of depression. Each time, when I was "found" once more, whatever form that experience of being found took, I felt the wonderous relief and energy of knowing who I was and where I was going and why, again. Being found is, indeed, as the hymn suggests, one of life's greatest blessings, well worth celebrating.

"I once was lost, but now I'm found." Former Episcopal priest Barbara Brown Taylor, in a series of reflections on spiritual practices in her book, *An Altar in the World*, makes the argument that being lost itself—not being found, but being lost—can be an important spiritual experience, the sort of experience worth seeking out from time to time. While she begins innocently enough describing getting lost on purpose on her drive to work or straying from the path while wandering around her farm, Taylor moves on to those experiences of lostness that knock the legs out from under us, scare us to death, remind us of how tentative life can be, how precarious our existence is, how little control we have over what happens. And then she has the temerity to celebrate the experience, saying:

> You are exquisitely vulnerable in this moment. You are vulnerable *to* this moment. Your carefully maintained safety net has ripped. Your expensive armor has sprung a leak. You are in need of help, and your awareness of this is not a bad thing .... There is something holy in this moment of knowing just how perishable you are. It is part of the truth about being human, however hard most of us work not to know that.

Think about your own times of being found, and ask yourself: could you summon the same response for your times of being lost? We have endured, are still enduring, an overwhelming time of being lost in a pandemic: will we ever sing passionately about this time, regard the pandemic as having been holy rather than the loss of all that was holy? Does the experience of being lost have its own intrinsic meaning, or is it only meaningful when it opens up into the experience of being found?

"I once was lost, but now I'm found." Spiritual traditions of all kinds are full of stories of being lost, so full one might conclude that the state or experience of lostness is part and parcel of a spiritual journey. Read from one perspective, the Hebrew Scriptures (the Biblical Old Testament), are basically a series of stories about individuals and communities who get lost over and over, and struggle to find a way out or a way home only to promptly get lost once more. Perhaps the best-known story of being lost is in Exodus, the account of the journey of the Hebrew people from being enslaved in Egypt to freedom; a journey that includes decades of wandering lost in the wilderness.

After the initial euphoria of being able to simply walk away from their suffering, the excitement of a sudden escape, and the amazement of the Red Sea crossing, reality set in for the Hebrews. How were they to survive in a harsh desert landscape with little or no provisions for food, with unpredictable access to water? Why did they sign on to such a journey without doing the careful research of determining whether this Moses person has what it takes to lead them? Where was the search team when it was time to fill this spot? When one is as seriously lost as the Hebrew people were at that moment, being captive back in Egypt might have looked good in comparison: an existence in which all the choices are already made, responsibility is taken by someone else, and nothing is left to chance.

So, the people began, not for the first time nor for the last time, to complain about Moses's lack of leadership skills, and to long for the familiar ways of the hard but predictable life they left behind in Egypt. And not for the first time nor for the last time, God stepped into the story in ways that demonstrate to the people that they do have all the resources they need if they can only trust enough to use them. This will be a lesson the people have to learn over and over again, a lesson in trust in their leaders and trust in their higher power to stick with them no matter how difficult the journey becomes, trust that life is not ultimately the barren desert it sometimes appears to be, trust that people can be moved by compassion to help, trust that hope and sacred power are present in every situation, no matter how dire.

"I once was lost, but now I'm found." This congregation, after many years of enjoying the place of being found, certain of your direction and purpose, has entered a time of wandering in the wilderness of transition. As was the case with all churches, you were first thrown into that wilderness by the pandemic that pushed all of us out of comfort and familiarity and into a place we had never seen, not even imagined. You brought your creativity and resources into play to figure out how to journey through that wilderness, only to have it prove to be longer and more unpredictable than envisioned. And to make matters harder, your pandemic wilderness has added into it the wilderness of a ministerial transition, a place where uncertainty and complicated questions about church priorities will surface on all sides in ways that make it hard to find a clear path.

As always happens in the course of such a wilderness journey, there are likely to be setbacks, and losses of people and resources. The experience of being found, of no longer feeling lost without a settled minister, is still a way off for you. So, like those Hebrew people, you will have to keep deciding: do you return to Egypt (if that is even possible), go back to the church you used to be and focus your energies on keeping that former church intact? Will you choose to just give up in the desert, use this transitional year to simply wait things out, until the search process brings your next minister? Or do you keep walking, continue the exhausting journey of transition of ministers and post-pandemic church, in the trust and hope that more life, more creativity, can still be discovered?

Barbara Brown Taylor rightly regards experiences of being lost in the wilderness as fundamental lessons in trust. She writes:

> The practice of getting lost has nothing to do with wanting to go there. It is something that happens, like it or not. You lose your job. Your lover leaves. The baby dies. At this point, the advanced practice of getting lost consists of consenting to be lost, since you have no other choice. The consenting itself becomes your choice, as you explore the possibility that life is for you and not against you, in spirt of all the evidence to the contrary.

Such trust is not something most of us are born with and can summon easily. It will require ongoing practice in order to deepen to the level where we can head off into the wilderness and know God will provide manna as needed, where we can ask strangers for help and believe they will respond with compassion, where we can risk congregational resources and be willing to fail as part of transforming the church, where we can sink into depths and trust that an everlasting love will be just as present in those depths as in the times of success and happiness.

"I once was lost, but now I'm found." I will always prefer being found and will likely always do everything I can to avoid being lost. I am someone who sets a high priority on remaining in control of my life at all times under any circumstances, so that lost experience of disorientation is a deep challenge for me. Yet here we are, you and I, heading off into the transition wilderness with projections and expectations and anxieties swirling around us, heading out to see whether we can work together in creative ways to build this beloved community that so engages us, and frustrates us, and cares for us, and calls us to be our best selves.

We are going to be lost for a time, probably longer a time than any of us wants. We will not get to sing "Amazing Grace" and celebrate being found, being lost no longer, for awhile. For now, being lost is our calling, and we are challenged to follow this calling with trust in ourselves, in one another, and in the sacred power that promises to be present whenever two or three come together. May we be willing to be lost and trust that with our willingness, we are already on the way to being found once more.

*Note: The service, "Lost," in which this sermon was delivered, was livestreamed on Sunday, September 19, 2021, at 9:00 a.m. To view the service, visit the Unity Church-Unitarian channel on YouTube, select the "Sunday Service" Playlist, and scroll down to find the date and title: www.youtube.com/c/unitychurchunitarian*

Community                                                          Joe Schur

*From the Pulpit*
**Aloha and Ohana**
**Rich Lau**

In Hawaii, there is a beloved local dish called chicken long rice, made from pieces of shredded chicken and strands of soft cellophane noodles, in a warm, savory, gingery broth, generously topped with green onions. Although it is not actually a native Hawaiian dish, it is a necessary part of any luau, as essential as kalua pig or poi.

There are several theories about the origin of chicken long rice. My favorite story takes place in the plantation days. The large agricultural farms that grew sugar cane and pineapple, during the late 19th and early 20th centuries, first used native Hawaiian labor, but the white plantation owners eventually brought in cheaper Chinese laborers. When the Chinese Exclusion Act of 1882 banned Chinese sojourners and immigrants, Japanese laborers were brought to Hawaii. They, in turn, were supplanted by even cheaper Filipino labor after US control of the Philippines gave the US a ready source of low-cost brown labor.

The racial and economic tensions between immigrant groups in the plantation camps were often tense. Competition, resentment, mistrust, and prejudice created segregated ethnic factions that occasionally flared into outright violence. Outside agitators, often displaced white laborers, frequently pitted one group against the other with rumors and deliberate misinformation. Hawaii was hardly paradise.

One evening, the story goes, some Filipino laborers were cooking chicken in a pot. Some hungry Hawaiians saw this and offered to contribute a portion of the sea salt they had harvested, in return for a share of the meal. Then some Chinese offered to contribute extra noodles and bits of ginger to the pot. Not wanting to be left out, Japanese laborers offered green onions and a portion of their short grain rice. The laborers put aside their suspicions about one another for an evening, shared what they had, and thereby created a warm, comforting, and delicious meal. Chicken long rice was invented.

I doubt the story is true, but I would like to believe it is. Eventually these diverse ethnic groups in Hawaii would lead to a confluence of foods and cultures, long before mainland chefs popularized the concept of fusion cuisine.

But culturally, native Hawaiians had a huge influence on how islanders treated each other. Disney's *Lilo & Stitch* taught movie-goers that "*ohana* means family and family means that no one gets left behind or forgotten," but the concept of ohana was already deeply ingrained in Hawaii. Beyond immediate family, ohana meant aunties, uncles, and cousins, almost to an infinite degree of distance. If you are auntie's nephew's cousin's sister-in-law's brother, you are ohana in Hawaii.

And you will be made to feel *aloha*, probably the best known and most misunderstood Hawaiian word.

Aloha is both a greeting and a farewell. It means love, kindness, peace, and compassion; literally, the breath of life. It is a way of being—living life in balance, harmony, and positivity toward others. And of acting, with sincere care, concern, and warmth, without any expectation in return. Aloha is not transactional. You feel aloha, you act aloha, you live aloha. The idea of aloha is so much a part of what it means to live in Hawaii that a 1986 state law requires state judges and government officials to treat the public with aloha.

Hawaiians also believe in *lokomaika'i*, the importance and obligation of treating each other with good will, generosity, kindness, and graciousness. It is one of the underlying principles of aloha. Hawaiians knew that one had to share from one's abundance to survive. In ancient Hawaii the larger islands were divided into districts, which were further divided into wedge-shaped tracts of land that ran from the mountains to the sea. In this way, each tract would have resources: hard volcanic rock for tools; high forest hardwood trees; freshwater streams and fertile land for cultivating vital crops; lowlands to raise chickens and pigs; and wide, broad access to the ocean for fishing and salt. Resources and abundance were shared, not bartered, so the community could thrive. Acting with lokomaika'i was acting *pono*, righteous. Pono, or right action, is another essential element of aloha.

This philosophy of the shared community is not so different from that of our spiritual ancestors. In his book, *The Myth of American Individualism*, contemporary scholar Barry Alan Shain quotes Congregationalist Minister Levi Hart and Presbyterian pastor and teacher Gilbert Tennant. In 1775 Hart preached that in a well-ordered society, "each individual gives up all private interest that is not consistent with the general good . . . and every individual is to seek and find his happiness in the welfare of the whole." And Tennant asserted that "we were born not merely for ourselves, but the Publick Good! which as Members of Society you are obligated *pro virili* [to the best of your ability] to promote."

Shain writes that for the committed reform Protestants at the time of the American Revolution, living without public spirit was equivalent to living without God, and that public spirit gave birth to the fundamentals of colonial, and then American, life: the public-school house, collective decision making for the benefit of the community in town hall meetings, subsidizing and building public infrastructure. Yet the myth, the lie, of rugged individualism persists and perniciously undermines some of the very things that bind us as Americans. It tells us that we don't need each other, we shouldn't need each other, and we certainly don't need to share with each other.

We know this is not true.

Our UU principles tell us that the good of the community is more important than individual ownership or achievement. We joined this church because we believe in the good of the community. Telling you to live aloha, well, that's like preaching to the choir.

We know we are better when we share our abundance. But do we share with everyone? Or just with our family and friends, and those with whom we are okay sharing?

According to the Bible, the Jews had a word, *shibboleth*, to identify who among their neighbors was actually Jewish. If you could pronounce the word correctly, then you were a member of the tribe and allowed to cross the river in peace. Do Unitarians have a shibboleth, a way to identify other Unitarians or like-minded people? When we see a Co-Exist or Penzeys bumper sticker on a Prius, do we greet them as family? Do we give someone wearing a vintage Wellstone T-shirt at the Saint Paul Farmers' Market a knowing nod?

The point being, do we have a password and are we more likely to share our abundance with "our" people? I can share abundance with my family, even my extended family. And I consider all of you my church ohana; I can share any abundance with you, even if I don't personally know you very well. But I struggle with the idea of sharing my abundance, much less my necessities, with people I don't like.

No one said being a UU was easy. Some critics maintain we pick and choose the parts that we like—a little Christianity here, a little Buddhism there, maybe a splash of Native American beliefs. This is wrong. We may look to other traditions for universal truths, but we have seven principles. Choosing to follow those principles does not "save" us or set us apart from others. There is no us and them. We don't share our abundance, or even our scarcity, only with those just like us. We don't have a shibboleth. Instead, we make a covenant to live lives of aloha, of lokomaika'i, to act with pono. To do what is right. No, my friends, it is not easy.

When I think of the origin story of chicken long rice, I imagine how difficult it would have been for the groups of Hawaiians, Chinese, Japanese, and Filipinos to overcome their feelings about one another, their mistrust and even hostility. It could not have been easy for them to share, even from their abundance, with those who were not like them. But I want to imagine that some people were brave enough to build a bigger table, and in doing so not only made something amazingly tasty to pass on to their descendants, but, in that moment, embraced living aloha, and expanded the idea of ohana.

May we be like them. May we be brave enough and strong enough to share our abundance with everyone. May we treat everyone with good will, generosity, kindness, and graciousness. May we live aloha. May it be so and amen.

*Note: This is an excerpt from a sermon delivered at Unity Church-Unitarian on Sunday, August 29, 2021. To view the service, which was livestreamed and recorded, visit the Unity Church-Unitarian channel on YouTube, select the "Sunday Service" Playlist, and scroll down to find the date and title: www.youtube.com/c/unitychurchunitarian*

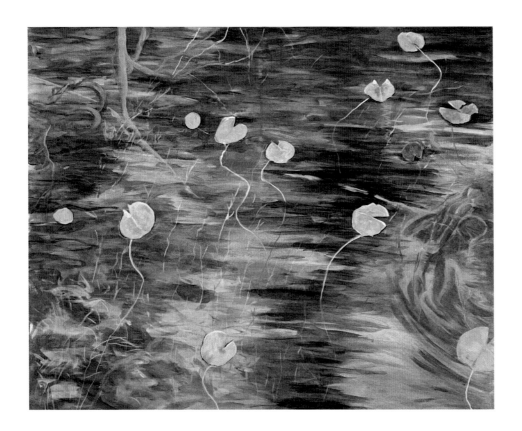

Above: Shallow Floaters 1
Below: Taking a Moment

Cynthia Starkweather-Nelson

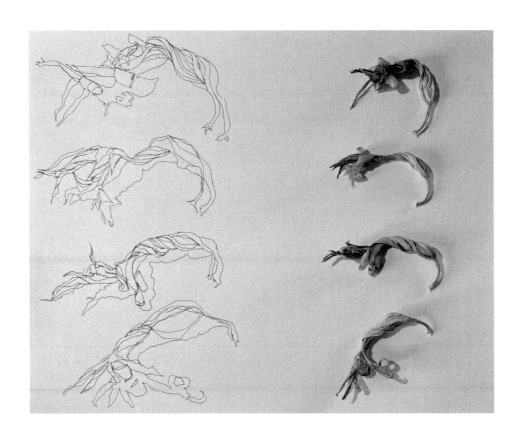

# ER
**Joe Schur**

"Patient arrival to triage, Rooms 4 and 21, please."

"PCA to mental health, please."

"Anesthetist in Room 23 in five minutes."

Does anyone listen to Muzak on a PA system? Of course the blending of the music and the sound bites on CNN blasting from the TV ("... officers discovered the bodies of five family members, suicide/murder is suspected..."), interrupted by the regular announcements of hospital emergency room business, is not easy to take in. Seven nursing students—young, fresh, dressed in deep purple or blue from neck to ankle, walking at about four miles per hour—move purposefully toward the elevators. The mostly older patients wait silently, many draped in double-folded white cotton hospital blankets from chin to over the shoe. The patients look at the floor, if they look at all. They are not dressed in purple or blue, something in them lacking.

"All offices clear," reports a hunky, thirty-something security guard to someone on the other end of his two-way radio. (This is the guard that watched me closely as I entered the ER, Black man throws suspicious gaze at white man.)

Another security guard approaches the security station, body mass index of forty plus. The second guard says to the first, pointing his finger at the computer monitor, "It's right there, can't you see it?"

The first guard replies, "I see it, I see it." A third guard walks briskly through the room; he carries a black briefcase, has a freshly pressed uniform, spit-shined shoes. He's on his way up.

John and his wife are not troubled about others overhearing their conversation. Still, with the din of Muzak, CNN, and the PA, I only get snippets, scraps. They skip through a magazine.

"I guess she was just lonely."

"That tree right there is a mango tree."

"That's like mom's trailer."

"Sheeeeet, that's an F-250."

"I paid seven dollars for the T-shirt."

John is a man of forty who dresses like it matters. His short-sleeve plaid shirt fits perfectly, not a wrinkle. His black beret might look pretentious on another man, but at six foot four, John looks distinguished, formidable. My bet: John is a "Johnnie Walker Black" man.

The perky admitting staff woman in blue calls "John" with practiced volume. He stands and walks towards the grey cubicle, walking with the stride of a basketball player: stable, steady, forceful. John's wife trails behind in a pretty print blouse of blue, white, and gold. Are her thick shoulders newly stooped? Worry does that. I'm betting John finally took her advice to come to the ER. Another bet: she's persistent.

John does not look right, sitting tall in the wheelchair. He refuses the blanket, politely. His wife folds her hands together at her waist, tightly. The wheelchair pusher puts her ID card near the reader on the always-locked, oversized swinging doors—loud click one. The door closes behind them—loud click two.

I remember my dad being in the ER, the last time he went. People shrink at some point, you know. John was still full-sized. Good luck, John.

Hong Kong 4                                                                 Robert Gestner

**Who to Write to Tonight?**
**Caroline Foster**

When you want to write to someone,
But you don't know who that is, give it thought.
It could be someone from the past,
Someone from the future you don't even know yet,
Or someone from the present day.
Take today, a mixed bag:
A pleasant visit with a neighbor,
Resulting in lost keys never recovered;
And a phone call to the wrong person.

The alternative to today was to stay in bed.

No, the visit was worth the lost keys,
And the phone call eventually reached the right Olson—
the doctor, not the recorder player.
My hubby brought home cookies that were too sweet...
I just had another one,
And now I still haven't written the perfect letter
To someone who wants a perfect letter, which I don't know how to do.

Maybe I should settle on "Dear God."

Time for bed.
On goes the nightgown, backwards,
Then turning it around. It's dark in the room and darker inside the gown.
Just another one of those days.

Shadow Play                                             Hilary Magnuson

A New Window on Lake Superior                                   Arlene West

## The Nice Little Two-Night Trip
**Dutton Foster**

God knows life isn't perfect, but occasionally
we take a little two-night trip and everything lines up in a charming way.
We encounter cool pleasant weather for the first bike ride,
which is all downhill coming back and ends right by
River Market with those nice sandwiches we eat by the river,
across which the big new bridge and big new four-lane
lead to a smaller curving two-lane and a turnoff at Church Road.
The cabin is a fun one, with a considerable ladder to the sleeping loft,
but you decide you'll sleep on the downstairs porch
to avoid dealing with that ladder in the night.
Your salads hit the spot and so does the wine, and we sing and
play a little music. Next morning, we paddle through lily pads
in a 17-foot Grumman just like the ones our dads owned,
while an osprey heads to its nest on a distant pole.
Our map shows us a nearby bike trail on a railroad grade
on which we remember riding a train before they tore up the track,
leaving it to goldfinches, orioles, and us. And wow, from the car we
see a pair of sandhill cranes with their chick camping along a creek.
Dinner in Osceola includes patio, catbird, and waterfall below.
Next morning a great blue heron and a nice brown thrasher appear,
but the cranes have left. We take our ritual coffee break
and language lesson as we drive toward home.
En route we take one more ride, on the Gateway trail,
passing three laughing horsewomen leading a foal.
No luck solving the Piano Puzzler on the way home,
but still, a very nice little 58th anniversary trip.

**It Was All My Fault**
**Neil Mikesell**

When I was little, our family went up north to a lake resort for vacation. Then, while I was in elementary school, we went up north to a lake resort for our getaway. Later, during junior and senior high school, we all piled into the car and drove up north to a lake resort to, as the Brits would say, "Go on holiday." However, one of these vacations, as it turned out, changed the course of my family's life, each and every one of us. And it was all my fault!

At the age of five or six, our family lived in a suburb of Chicago, Tinley Park. For either Christmas or my birthday, I can't recall which, I asked for a fishing pole, reel, and tackle set from a toy catalogue. The following summer, on our trip up north to a lake resort for our vacation, which was in those years in Michigan, the opportunity came to finally use the gift that my parents had given me. While my memory of the actual occasion is vague, the memory of the result and subsequent story is not.

With every cabin rental at that particular resort, came a small aluminum rowboat. The day came! My father took me, my fishing gear, and some worms, and rowed out on the lake. I got to fish for the first time! Then the unthinkable happened: I caught a fish, and not just any fish. It was a three and one-half pound smallmouth bass, the largest fish caught that week at the resort. I caught the fish but, as you might expect, my father reeled it in. Immediately upon our return to the resort, he went out and bought a real rod and reel, a landing net, some tackle, and a small tackle box. Much of the rest of our stay was spent out on the lake.

Soon after, Dad decided that the fishing in Michigan wasn't good enough, so we went up north to a lake resort in Minnesota for our vacation. During these years, he worked for 3M in the Chicago area, so the next logical step was to apply for a transfer to a 3M plant in Minnesota. So it was that at the end of my fourth-grade year, our family moved to Shoreview, MN, a suburb of St. Paul. During the summers, we would go up north to a lake resort for our vacation where we would rent a cabin with a boat along with a small outboard motor and spend much of the time out on the lake, fishing.

Except for two years right after college, all of my life after leaving Chicago I have lived in Minnesota. I think by now, it is fair to call myself a Minnesotan. I came here for possibly, the most Minnesota of reasons, fishing. It wasn't my choice, but you see, it's all my fault and that of a smallmouth bass.

My America                                                                                                    Kathryn Oakley

**The Order of Things**
**Daphne Thompson**

Betty was standing by the window, looking across the field of dry weeds and lumped furrows. On the other side was the ice cream stand, a white box just visible a block away. She wanted a cone. It was an eight-year-old's obsession on a hot afternoon. "Can we go get a Tastee Freeze?" she asked Mom.

"Well, sure, if Daphne will go with you."

I scrunched up my nose. "I don't want one," I said. "It's 95 degrees out there. I'm not going." At twelve, I was the oldest.

Betty said, "Please, Mom. I'll go. Jackie can go with me. We can do it. Pleeease!" Mother looked across the field, then back at Betty's pleading eyes.

Five-year-old Jackie was hopping up and down trilling, "A coh-ohn. A coh-ohn."

Finally, Mom said, "Well, I think it'll be all right. You need to hold Jackie's hand, though, and cross at the corner, with the light."

Betty nodded, "Don't worry, I will." She accepted the two dimes offered and they went out the front door, chattering about which flavor they wanted.

There were two ways to the Tastee Freeze. The shortest way was directly across the field, kitty-corner to the ice cream place. The second, much longer, was to walk a half-block, turn left, and walk the full block to the store.

Betty chose the short way.

I stood with Mom at the window, watching their progress and thinking about the cone I wouldn't get. I was impressed by the dimes; usually we just got a nickel. Ten feet into the field, I could see that Jackie was in trouble. She had stopped, looking up at Betty, and even through the glass, we could hear her howls.

"Huh!" I snorted. "She didn't even take her sandals!" Everyone knew the field was full of stickers. Even the toughest kids wouldn't walk barefoot through them. Betty should have known better than to take her like that. Now they would have to come back. Maybe I'd go with them this time.

Instead, Betty leaned down and Jackie climbed up on her back. Her arms went around Betty's neck and Betty locked her arms around Jackie's knees. They started off again. Fifteen steps later, Betty was looking back over her shoulder at the house. I knew she could see us in the window. She hitched Jackie up on her back and took a few more steps. Again, the turn; again, the look.

After the third turn-back, Mom cleared her throat. "Daphne."

"Oh, all right," I grumped. "I'll go. But why do I always have to be the one?" I pictured the cone I was going to order.

"Here's a dime for you," she said.

"Thank you!" I slid the dime into the pocket of my orange plaid shorts, buckled on my own sandals, and ran outside.

Mother called to me, "Don't you want Jackie's shoes?"

"That's OK," I said, hurrying to the rescue across the blacktopped street and into the stubble of the field.

Betty turned at the slam of the front door. Her grin was immediate. She offered her burden to me, but I made her hold Jackie while I inspected her feet, pulling out a few sticker spines before letting her climb on my back. My shirt bunched under her as she crawled on and I felt warm hands around my neck.

Betty launched a celebratory dance. She skipped and hopped across the field as I called, "Why didn't you make her wear her sandals?"

The Tastee Freeze grew closer. "You're just lucky I'm here, that's all I can say." I fingered the dime in my pocket. I was going to get a big cone! "I *always* have to be the one," I raised my voice to Betty's prancing back, which was now ten yards ahead of me.

Jackie slipped. "Hang on, Jackie," I grumbled. "You have to help me. I can't do everything!" She scooched back up, tightening her arms around my neck.

I had a new thought: "I could get a chocolate dip!" Saliva glands twanging under my chin, I remembered how melted chocolate hardens on cold ice cream.

We were almost there. "Wait for me at the street, Betty! You know you have to wait for me," I bossed. She took three more skips and stopped cheerfully on the curb.

Closing the last twenty feet between us, I huffed irritably, "All right then, take my hand." She did, and sprang up and down until I snapped, "Will you quit jumping around?"

We crossed the street and I put Jackie down. Betty skipped to the window. I growled, "Boy, you two should just be glad I took you. I didn't even want to come here!"

Jackie sang, "I-scream, I-scream." Betty took up her dance again, bouncing and spinning in the shade under the store awning. And I? My hand was around the dime in my pocket and I was the first in line.

**Daphne Thompson**
**Sisters**

Some sisters are close and
some as far apart as spite.
Still, they finish each other's sentences,
agree on the ways of their mother,
and answer the phone in her voice.

I wanted to sock one sister
half my life, and she, me.
But we all took care of Mom
when she needed it.
"You're a good daughter,"
means a lot from a sister
when you've lost it with your aging mother,
who's just gone inexplicably sharp.

She's tired; you're already lonely.
Only your sisters know.
They stood with you
with their arms around her
after your father's funeral.
Three sad half-orphans, crying,
"Don't you die, we need you,"
trying to call her back.

Plus, they're the last ones, really,
who still like to see the old home movies,
who can do them four hours at a stretch,
bringing back the days when Dad would build a fire,
pop corn, and we'd all hole up in the loft,
watching our two and five and nine-year old
images dance in the living room, or,
do a Swan in shoes and skating costumes
on the front lawn before the show.

I like to watch sisters in airports, and shopping.
There's something comforting,
even when they fight in public.
"We'd never do that," I think smugly.
And then I see the hand on the shoulder,
the wink, and hear their laughter
rising in harmony from the family vocal cords.

The children and their spouses say we all talk at once,
chattering away at top speed and volume
to the amusement of the new daughter-in-law.

She has sisters too.

Instinctive                                                    Peggy Wright

**Tales from My Un-Careers**
**Kathryn Oakley**

Do you remember the first jobs you had as a teenager, the ones that showed you what you definitely *didn't* want to do when you grew up? I've come to think of those jobs as our "un-careers"; they introduce us to the work world and teach us a lot. I'd like to share a few experiences from *my* un-careers.

**Sister Edna's Teeth**

My first post-babysitting job, at fifteen, was bequeathed to me by a friend who was moving on to something bigger and better. I was hired to assist a one-chair dentist working out of a seedy little office above a drugstore. Poor Dr. McTooth, I soon learned, had recently returned from treatment for alcoholism and the restoration of his license to practice. He was a kindly enough fellow, although his inner office smelled strongly of chain-smoking and despair. He taught me the rudiments of dental assisting: handing him picks, probes, and mirrors; developing x-rays; mixing silver fillings; and autoclaving instruments.

Things went well enough for a while. I liked wearing my cute white uniform and feeling like a real medical professional. As time went on, though, I became concerned about the help I was providing without much background. This came to a head the day one of my sixth-grade Catholic school teachers showed up, with a companion nun, to have "some" of her teeth pulled.

Sister Edna was stoic while Dr. McTooth lowered her back in the chair, clipped on the white napkin, and administered several shots of Novocain. He then proceeded to yank out EIGHT of her top teeth. She groaned in pain as the extractions mounted and her mouth absolutely filled with blood. Dr. Mc-Tooth called for more and more cotton dental rolls, which I breathlessly handed to him as fast as I could. He finally got the bleeding stopped. Poor Sister Edna struggled to her feet, cheeks bulging with cotton, and staggered out of the office, assisted by her companion. I wondered if we'd done right by her.

I'd like to say these ethical concerns led to my resignation, but it was self-interest that eventually prevailed. Dr. McTooth had only a light grasp of the clerical work needed to support a practice. I tried to help, but I couldn't pay myself. Every two weeks I had to remind him it was payday. With a deep sigh, he'd pull out his checkbook, ask me how many hours I'd worked, and write me a check, sometimes not for the full amount. I decided my days of amateur dental assisting must come to an end.

But I had learned:

- Entry-level assistant and clerical skills;
- How to speak up when I hadn't been paid fairly; and
- That cotton will absorb almost any amount of unchecked bleeding.

## Popcorn Girl

The same friend who'd directed me toward Dr. McTooth's office was now leaving her next job, staffing the one-person concession stand at a small movie theater in Minneapolis. I applied for and was offered the job. From 5:00 p.m. to midnight, I presided over the little concession alcove, keeping the candy counter stocked, and making (very good!) popcorn in the automated popper. A stainless-steel butter machine on the counter dispensed real butter, warm and melted, for the popcorn.

The job was fairly easy and pleasant; it was fun to watch the movie customers and fill their simple orders at the counter. The manager, Tim, a rather slick fellow in his 30s, didn't come around much, although he was a source of moral indignation to my young Catholic self: an usher told me that Tim, who was married and the father of two, had a girlfriend on the side that he brought to the theater sometimes.

I'd been there for most of the summer when two incidents involving Tim made me decide to look for another job. One evening, he entered the tiny concession space and stood behind me while I waited on customers. To my shock, he began to repeatedly run his finger down my back from my hairline to my waist, in such a way that the customers couldn't see it, but I could definitely feel it. Today, if anyone tried that maneuver on me, he'd experience a quick elbow to the gut or a bone-crunching step on his foot, but I was too young and scared to respond. I think I may have only said, "Hey!" He left.

It didn't happen again. But then came The Butter Incident, about a week later. One of my first duties each day was to remove the stainless-steel bowl of popcorn butter from the fridge and put it into the butter machine to warm. The butter bowl was only emptied and washed once a month; butter was added each day to whatever was still in the bowl from the previous day. This day, however, I discovered scores of tiny red ants busily crawling through the butter. My automatic response was to scrape the ant-infested butter into the trash.

Manager Tim popped through the door just as I was getting started. "What are you doing?!!"

"Scraping out the butter bowl. It's full of ants!"

"No, no, no!" he exclaimed. "We just do this." He took the bowl from me, found a paring knife in a drawer, and began picking the ants out of the butter. When he'd eliminated most of them, he handed the bowl back to me to insert into the butter machine. "Butter is expensive! We don't throw out a big bowl of it like that." He stomped out. A few days later, I handed in my resignation.

But I had learned:

- Beginning customer service skills;
- That, unlike the men I'd grown up around, some guys could be real jerks toward women; and
- You should always check out the butter sanitation arrangements at your local theater.

**Disaster in Short Order**

I found out the local drugstore needed a part-time waitress and short-order cook. I can't imagine what possessed me to think I was the right person for the job. I was sixteen, tall and uncoordinated, with culinary skills stretching from popcorn to chocolate chip cookies and not beyond.

My job was to take the orders, and then cook and serve them as well. There were usually one or two other waiters/cooks on duty, as well as our supervisor, Ruby.

Ruby was cut along classic waitress lines: trim, fortyish, hair teased and lacquered in a high French twist. She was sharp-tongued, peppy, and no-nonsense. I admired her mightily, and failed almost totally to perform to her exacting standards.

As always, I meant well. But I'd get confused about how the Junior Executive (two eggs scrambled, three sausage links, toast, jam, coffee) differed in price from the same items ordered a la carte with orange juice, and I was constantly having to consult the menu. This slowed me down considerably as I caromed in confusion between counter and kitchen.

Then, too, I was hampered by shyness and a deep inclination to let people make their own decisions.

"Now here's what we do, honey," Ruby explained. "When somebody sits down at the counter and orders a cup of coffee and nothing else, we suggest."

"Suggest?" I asked weakly.

"'How about a doughnut with that, sir?'"

"'Our apple pie is fresh this morning. Would you like a piece with your coffee?' We get a bigger sale and, of course, a bigger tip. See?"

"Sure," I answered.

But I couldn't do it. At first, I'd flat out forget, focused on filling the coffee cup without spilling. Later I ventured a timid "How 'bout a doughnut?" to a few mild-mannered businessmen. They cast an eye over our tired selection of pastries and declined.

Ruby took my natural reticence hard. She didn't give up easily, though. As she swept behind me at the counter with her loaded trays, she'd elbow me in the back and hiss, "Suggest! Suggest!" But I rarely did.

Have you ever watched a short-order cook in action? Slap, slap, two burgers on the grill. Flip! Two buns buttered and added. Peel off two slices of bacon from the slab in the fridge and throw them on the grill. Butter six slices of bread, four white, two whole wheat. Scoop of tuna, scoop of tuna, scoop of egg salad. Lettuce, lettuce, hold the lettuce, tomato. Flip the burgers, turn the bacon. Break three eggs into the sizzling fat, deftly scramble with the big stainless-steel spatula. Halve the sandwiches, add potato chips, pickles. Next order.

I learned a lot in a hurry, but not fast enough. My efforts came to a horrifying climax one Sunday morning when a booth of four customers ordered a complex array of items. After too long, I served the exasperated group rubbery scrambled eggs, hot bacon, cold toast, half frozen hash browns, and coffee I couldn't keep warm as I dashed back and forth. They stared at me while they paid the bill. I was mortified, but not surprised, when, clearing the table after they left, I found the napkin on which they'd written, "This is the worst breakfast we ever ate!"

A day or two later Ruby took me aside after the lunch rush and said, "Honey, I don't think you were cut out for this. Leave your apron and cap by the back door."

In a fog of humiliation, I left for the bus home, crying until I was halfway to the stop. Then it dawned on me: I never had to go back there again! I boarded the bus smiling broadly.

I had learned so many things:

- Short-order cooking is an art; respect and praise its artists, of which I am not one;
- Being fired is not the worst thing that can happen to you; and
- If pursuing a career in marketing, maximize sales by cross-selling products: "Suggest! Suggest!"

### Epilogue

There were a few more un-career jobs over the years before I found my niche in teaching. I don't regret them. They made me grateful for the variety of talents we humans possess. And they certainly provide me with plenty of rueful laughs every time I remember them.

**Dual-Retirement Gifts to Ourselves: A Pair of Palindromes**
**Mary E. Knatterud**

Our new dual-retirement gifts to ourselves don't ever
let a voicemail go unheard for days,
let weeks go by without a promised Zoom or FaceTime,
let my hurt face at a snarky aside stay in free fall,
let months elapse without returning a call,
let a friendship curdle over disparate COVID precautions,
let a heartfelt email or text languish unacknowledged,
let loose any ageist or sexist or racist remarks.

Au contraire, our new palindromic gifts let us
let go of the lopsided negotiations over loving contacts in the midst of delta
and simply paddle away from it all
out onto a sublime nearby lake
(well, once past the shoreline green slime,
the gross endless swaths of lily pads—
made grotesquely worse by climate change—
that preclude fishing on a dock past the end of May
that even a rowboat motor couldn't churn away).

But once on the shimmering open water, social-distanced and safe,
we swap out simmering anxiety and angst
for quiet activity and awe,
catching warm rays and wriggling sunnies
as egrets and herons strut
and owls hoot.
Contentedly perched, respectively,
in our Pelican Argo and L.L.Bean Manatee,
blue-green and orange and polyethylene,
we're full of unspoiled peace and Caribou,
serenely grateful for the Inuits who made *their* kayaks
with whalebone and oiled seal or caribou skins.

**Turning Seventy**
**Carol Mahnke**

I am now the oldest member of both my father's and my mother's families. I've gone from cherished first grandchild to withered old crone in just under seventy years. I get mail from crematoriums, insurance companies, and funeral homes. And the evidence is clear: I have more creases than laugh lines and my hair is turning white. I need my glasses for reading, and I walk slowly, with increasing chronic pain.

Until recently, I have been at an age that was difficult for people to guess, and people invariably guessed my age as less than it is. I liked that. No shortage of vanity here! But guesses are creeping closer to reality.

I try to keep as much in shape as someone pushing seventy can. Every weekday morning, I walk in the Vortex (that is, against the current) at the Midway YMCA. I walk with friends in regional parks weekly, and with my dog around the neighborhood daily.

And I actually feel better than I have through decades of chronic, often severe, depression. That is no small victory, and I owe it to the people at Unity Church-Unitarian and to the Vortex. But if it were up to me, I would rather be turning thirty than seventy (without the decades of depression ahead, of course).

I hate when people say, "It is what it is." But it is.

Being in my sixties seemed like being "almost" old. Seventy is the real thing.

Fears grow like gathering gloom. What if my forgetfulness is the beginning of dementia? I've always stumbled over words and forgotten names, and so far, I don't think there's any alarming change. There is family history, though, and I'm worried.

What if I fall and break my hip—or if I become too ill to take care of myself? Recently my sister, who is eighteen months younger than I am, fell and broke bones in both knees, but she is recovering well. Of course, she's still in her sixties.

What if I have to spend my waning years by myself? Well, I do, because my husband died five years ago. I'm handling life alone pretty well, with help from family and Unity friends. But in the coming years I will undoubtedly lose my constant companion—a chubby, black-and-tan dachshund named Gracie. She's in good health, but she is fourteen years old. Most of all I fear losing my independence.

Already a son is encouraging me to give up the keys to my KIA Soul. I learned to drive from my father on city streets and highways, and I do a fair amount of darting in and out of traffic. My son isn't the only one who doesn't want to ride with me. My car is ten years old but has only 80,000 miles on it, and I intend to put on many more miles!

I especially dread the prospect of losing the ability to care for myself. I cared for elderly people as a nurses' aide while I was in high school, and I can't think of a more personal invasion of privacy. I don't want to need that care myself.

I want to hang on long enough to write a memoir of my struggle with depression now that it has a happier ending. I survived some twenty hospitalizations and three courses of electro-convulsive therapy. There were years of counseling—some good, some not so much—and group therapy.

Still, I look with trepidation at the threshold of turning seventy. I'm aware that many people have gone through this advanced rite of passage without histrionics, but I have legitimate concerns. One in five of us will suffer dementia and the future is fraught with accidents and illness—else what would we have to talk about?

But there are also beautiful blue October skies and brilliantly colored leaves in autumn, pristine white blankets of new snow in winter, the rebirth of nature in spring, and those warm summer afternoons.

There's family to enjoy—for me, a grandson to watch grow, sons and a daughter-in-law, and sisters to visit. There are surprises big and small—and some will be good surprises.

I may be seventy, but I'm not ready to give up yet. Just worried.

## There Is That Grief
## Kim Chapman

There is that grief that is electric
    —the Haviland kid zig-zagging
    over the yards, arms straight
    and angled down, mouth
    in a cracked wail, at the moment
    his mother backed over the family dog.
That all made sense, the burst
    of anguish, wet cheeks, and
    our need to look away
    and leave them with their private
    momentary misery.
And then there is that other kind,
    the one you glimpse just over the hill,
    tracking you at a distance
    as you thread your way past, around and over
    the broken monuments
    to past imponderable events
    and people left behind
    —all the debris of living—all those
    decisions and roads not taken,
    the crisis moment weathered,
    but not well enough to spare you its regrets.
That kind of grief is not so different
    than the unpredicted tidal wave,
    signaling its approach with
    the slightest climb up the ocean beach,
    then a noticeable withdrawal
    down the naked shingles of your world,
    until you hear—or maybe only
    think you hear—the sound
    a tower of water makes
    as it falls, rebuilds itself, and falls again,
    approaching where you stand
    but still out of sight—and you know, you know
      as you know your own heartbeat
        and hidden thoughts, it will,
          very soon, be here.

**The Room**
**Kim Chapman**

Now that the floorboards of this house
have buckled under years of use—unnoticed
under shoe-worn tiles, the woven rugs
and furnishings that framed our lives—
we understand too late how much depended on
the steady voices of the ones who went before,
which they themselves had heard when young
and those before had listened to and taken in
as something of a birthright not to be resisted
nor written off as archaic hearsay,
but rather the true measure of what it is to be alive.

Too late now to winnow seed from chaff.
Too late to wish that more were made of moments past.
It is all past, that supple time of learning.

And now we stand in that beautiful room
that decades-long delighted us,
in which our loves were made or lost,
our friendships deepened or allowed to slip away,
mistakes played out, then brought to rights and forgiven—
but really, only healed by time's forgetting—
and all the glory that we craved and sometimes earned,
and all the kindnesses we gave or got by grace...
it all, the all of that, depended on and came
from them—the recent dented carpet and the slanting tiles
now understood as evidence and proof
of what they were to us—our frantic patchwork
of gestures layered on not really what our charge
in all that time had been—to lay for those to come
the undergirding of that room that would be theirs
when we at last stepped through the corner door,
always there but diligently ignored.

Survivor                                    Dutton Foster

## Tabula Rasa
## Cynthia Orange

It is autumn. We tell time by shortened day. Blazing leaf. Browning cornstalk. The cheers of soccer fans at the athletic field down the street rise and fall. Rise and fall. The sound of autumn breathing.

Soon, I'll need to get a new date book. It has become an important ritual ever since the year my cousin Chris died. I shop carefully, examining each sample. I feel the texture of the pages, look at the pictures, read the text; do all that is necessary to find the perfect book to hold my days, my life.

I often choose Georgia O'Keeffe Engagement Calendars. A page contains a week of rectangular blocks, one block for each day. Opposite the page of days is an O'Keeffe painting or a quote about her or her work. In the midst of notations about her life, I chart my own life. I record anniversaries, birthdays, death days.

Chris died April 6. The painting for that week is O'Keeffe's *Black Hollyhock, Blue Larkspur.* One huge, round, black hollyhock with a stark white, star-shaped center overwhelms the smaller blossoms of blue larkspur. But my eyes are drawn to the white star that emerges, like hope, from the dark petals.

While I let myself review past days, I try not to look ahead. I do not study the paintings or read the descriptions of O'Keeffe and her work until that week is over. It is my gift, my reward, for having lived all the days on the page, like uncovering the picture of Hopalong Cassidy at the bottom of my childhood cereal bowl when I ate all my oatmeal.

My preoccupation with datebooks really took hold when Chris was dying. With only weeks to live, she became obsessed with getting a Day-Timer—one of those elaborate appointment systems that comes bound in a fake-leather, zippered case. Cancer had spread to her brain and spine, and she spent most of her days in the hospital bed her husband Al had set up in their living room so she could still be part of the pulse of the house. She directed the household goings on from that bed like an ebullient conductor, waving her little porcelain bell like a baton.

Chris was forty-five the year she died. She was a large woman. Her straight, dark hair had fallen out from chemo, and her scalp was soft with downy new growth. Chris' mother (my Aunt Margaret) kept a constant vigil those last months, bathing her daughter every day and massaging lotion tenderly onto her body. An anointing. Then Aunt Margaret would dress Chris in bold red fleece sweats or a bright flowered duster. There was nothing subtle about my cousin.

She'd sit in bed, clean and neat, propped up against pillows, studying catalogs and Sunday ads, looking for the perfect datebook. One weekend when I was visiting, I heard her bell's insistent "Ring/ring/ring/ring/ring," and "Cathy? Are you still here? I *need* to see your datebook." Aunt Margaret, my cousin Cathy, and I rushed from three different directions to her bedside. After Chris examined her sister's book, she demanded to see all of our calendars. We obliged, rustling through purses, briefcases, and pockets, handing them over like weapons at a gun bust. She liked Cathy's best, and decided she needed to buy one like it. IMMEDIATELY. It was Sunday afternoon in Boone, Iowa, and the stores would close soon.

"Mom, hand me my wig, please. Cathy, don't forget the handicap tag. I haven't had a chance to use it yet. We'll get to park right by the door!"

As Chris brightly ticked off her list of items for the shopping expedition—photo albums for each of her four boys, a new blue fleece outfit, and, of course, the datebook—we moved her wheelchair to her bedside. The growth of tumors in her spine had weakened her legs, so it was difficult for her to move. While I steadied the wheelchair, Cathy helped Chris hoist herself into it.

Chris wore a satisfied look when she and Cathy returned from the shopping trip. Chris was energized. Cathy was exhausted. They had driven thirty miles to K-Mart for the Day-Timer. The bound book was fat with possibility: pages for notes, and pockets for lists, prescription slips, reminders. Pages on which Chris could dissect her days—slice them into pieces divided by hours. She hugged it to her chest for a silent moment, looking absolutely content.

Then she sprang back into action, impatient to get back into bed to begin work on her new Day-Timer. Al put his arms out to give Chris a firm bear hug as she placed her arms on his shoulders so that she could raise herself out of the wheelchair. They took the few steps toward the bed in an awkward but sweet little "shuffle dance," and after Al positioned Chris so she could sit comfortably with her legs dangling over the edge of the bed, we fluffed her pillows to support her back and wheeled the bedside table over.

Chris tossed her wig aside, rubbed her smooth head, and pulled the table up closer. She carefully removed the book from its wrapper and studied the loose advertising and information pieces that came with it. She filled out a form for free inserts and asked me to find a stamp so the request could be mailed first thing Monday morning. Just across from the corner where the stamp was to go were the bold and taunting words: "Allow four to six weeks for delivery." I pinched the stamp and card hard between my thumb and finger, then buried the card in the pile of outgoing mail.

Chris opened her new Day-Timer like we were taught to open new textbooks in elementary school, carefully loosening the spine by gently flattening the pages. She recorded every date she remembered: meetings with the funeral director, the hospice nurses' visits, her kids' birthdays, their schedules. Tabula rasa no longer. The blank slate was getting filled in.

Chris looked like a Buddha sitting there, serene and focused, head bowed over her book. As she wrote, recording her days in lavender ink, I saw life emerging from the empty pages. There was movement—the blessed movement of life being lived. Time that had been paralyzed by the darkness of cancer, pain, and morphine moved haltingly, then boldly forward.

Purpose, intent, *and* defiance flowed onto each page, into each moment, filling the spaces, like breath.

Hosta 'Guacamole' Triptych                                        Paul Rogne

**Immortality**
**Richard Buggs**

A simple, wooden coffin,
cautiously lowered
through drought-dry earthen
walls into its final place
of rest. The rabbi
offering a Hebrew chant,
invoking reverent farewells.
Mike's family first, each
shoveling dirt onto
the coffin, the shovel
backside up, a gesture
of mourning,
front side up, a
gesture of acceptance.

Shoveling dirt,
striking in its simplicity,
a liturgy beyond words.
The pile of dry earth
beside the open grave
reduced slowly,
shovel by shovel,
an earthen sentinel
guarding his return
to dust beginnings.

As mourners comfort
with quiet conversation,
the rhythmic shoveling,
becomes its own chant,
each shovel full
tapping the coffin
with whispers of gratitude
for the gift of Mike,
our memories,
his guaranteed
immortality.

**Mending**
**Richard Buggs**

I can still see her seated
by the window,
a worn sock in hand,
light bulb pushed inside,
giving the beaten sock
a taste of reincarnation.

Spotting a matching color
in her sewing box,
she'd slide the selected thread
through her lips,
moist for a precision
needle-hole strike.

Mending began,
usually a toe,
sometimes an abused heel,
threaded needle gliding
back and forth,
a soothing rhythm,
arousing an inner calm,
humming gratitude
to this ritual of reverent repair.

What she knew
nowadays dismissed
as boring drudgery:
simple tasks of daily repair
can become rituals of soul repair,
lifting one out of the
noise of daily hubbub
into the calming sweetness
of balance restored.

**Pedaling Solo**
**Richard Buggs**

After an hour or so,
the sailing begins,
moving effortlessly,
mind empty,
body feeling absent,
just the essence of me
moving in the breeze,
feeling its quiet touch,
how it taps my
cheeks differently than
it licks my neck.
Sailing along,
silent, on my own power,
feeling ageless,
cerebral monkey talk
dropped back there
someplace, lying
now dehydrated
on the trail.
Pedaling into
and through each
second. It's pure
magic, how the
splendor of "just being"
can be touched by
pedaling solo.

**Exuberance**
**Richard Buggs**

Inflated by life's abundance,
a wild, color-packed impulse,
always unannounced,
demanding a shout,
a sidewalk jig, a YIPPIE.

Fact: exuberance triggers
conflicting emotions—
welcomed in children,
distrusted in teen years,
disparaged in adulthood.
There are, of course,
exceptions: exuberance
following an athletic victory, a
little madness after a few drinks,
etc. For this,
a cultural thumbs up!!

Embraced exuberance,
luminescence on a dark day,
a booster shot for
a spirit parched by duty.
Thwarted exuberance,
a lost resurrection,
an eruption of wild, neon colors beat
down in favor of shades of gray.

Waxing Crescent Moon                              Richard Birger

**Big George**
**Barbara Nicholson**

Monster
of a man
only
in stature

standing
he blacks out
all scenery
behind him

stage floor
shudders
under the
rhythmic
stomp of
size 18
shoes

must sit
to play
age and
disease
demand
his legs

harmonica
fused
to his fist
eyes closed
every
shout and
response
rattles
the chains
of memory

only by singing
the blues
can you
defeat them
he directs to
the well-traveled face
in the front row
knowing
she has been here
before

breathing hard
he takes a break
sliding
into the chair
beside her

with
surprising
grace

his massive
hand
engulfs
both of hers

he smiles
I see you really
dig my music
he whispers
so talk to me
woman.

*Dedicated to Big George Jackson—1950-2021*

**Fabric**
**Barbara Nicholson**

Loving him
was like
satin
silky slick
so easy
to slip
in and out
of my arms

Loving you
is being wrapped
in fine
worsted wool
warm
resilient
ready to rebuff
those cold spells
that love
invents

I am finally
dressed
for the
whether.

**Not What I Look Like**
**Daphne Thompson**

He thinks I am what I look like:
the almost fifty woman
in a business suit.

This new man sees
a capitalist, a conservative,
or help me, a conformist?

Can't he see the ex-hippie,
the raging pacifist, reformed drunk
who still peer mocking from my eyes?

I once wore kaftans and headbands,
long hair swinging; or later, with
masses of curls lifting in the breeze.

Radical feminist attire allowed
anything you wanted to wear, if—
you wore it angry.

Then tired of that, I wanted to
laugh again, bite an apple in joy,
and quit grinding my teeth.

At thirty-nine, I jogged,
re-wired time for voice lessons,
bought my first new car.

Later, back in Minnesota,
invested in some suits
and got a job.

It's just a *costume,* I think,
a business costume.
I'm not the act, I'm the actor.

Bridge Works                                                          Natasha Rodich

**Notes from a Meeting**
**Richard Hamer**

Lower the expectations
Targeted improvements are best
We can give something
And have the capacity to decide.
Teach the young
How this means everything
Maybe someday they can too.

When we are part of things
We have something to lose
Don't be rude
I'll call it rude
If you bring it up that way, I'll call it rude
We have a language, and
A way to use it.

Here are some concrete steps
Education, health, utilities,
And, also incarceration...
You shouldn't have to earn your opportunities
That is absurd
Let's operate in a different way
We can't have it two ways.

Hey, I'm willing to sacrifice my place
I'll think of them in a different way
Better yet, let's use an algorithm
That will be fair, let machines decide
They have no intentions, they don't know
With this we can chip away
Some can have direct deposit.
But really, don't get excited
Lower the expectations

We need thoughtful program design
Here's $25 if you do this
My words will not align with your experience
But here's $25 in any case
You'll have to work to get it
But here's $25
A rebate for your behavior.

Just today, I had an experience
Where I realized
He and I were not having the same experience
Things can look a little bit different, I guess

I'd like to get the conversation started
And write a case study
I want to talk about what I think and feel...

AND OPEN THINGS UP THAT WAY

I'm learning to be deliberate
People are well-intentioned
I've decided to seek input
Decisions are based on many
The more attuned
The more influence I'll have.

What are my reactions and assumptions when
I look at a person of color
In terms of a slightly bigger picture?
I'm practicing conversations
But there isn't any real contact
Only a grammar of opportunities
What can I do, What can I do?

## The Poetry of CIA Director John Brennan, December 11, 2014
## Richard Hamer

Our program produced useful information.

> Enhanced Interrogation Techniques may have produced useful information.

Or they may not have.

> There is no way of knowing.

Useful information was gained from persons who experienced
Enhanced Interrogation Techniques.

> But there is no way of knowing.

Would the revelations have occurred anyway?

Could the revelations have been obtained in another way?

Did the Enhanced Interrogation Techniques cause the useful information
to be revealed that day?

> These things are not knowable.

*Note: This poem was inspired by CIA Director John Brennan's response on December 11, 2014, to a Senate report on the use of Enhanced Interrogation Techniques, also known as torture, when dealing with prisoners from Iraq and elsewhere.*

Uprooted Tree in Crosby Park                    Jane Thomson

## Memorial Day
## Bill Quist

My town climbed aboard the patriotic bandwagon and dragged the band along with it. Yes, River Falls, Wisconsin, constructed a Veterans Memorial, and the high school band was conscripted to march in the parade to the dedication ceremony. The band students were literal draftees, having been informed their final grade in band class would be based on their participation.

A few years earlier, in the weeks leading up to the second invasion of Iraq, our son had marched the streets of River Falls in protest along with his parents and a group of other more-or-less sane individuals. To those of us who remembered Vietnam it was déjà vu: old white men telling us it was our duty to kill people halfway across the world in the interest of national security.

Our civic leaders were now telling the students they needed to march for a different reason: to honor those who served our country to protect our freedoms, such as they are. So, the River Falls Marching Wildcats bravely took their position on the street behind two surviving combat veterans of WWII, and a handful from Korea, Vietnam, Iraq I, Afghanistan, and Iraq II. The unwilling led by the misguided. A grand parade.

The procession began at the American Legion Hall and followed a course through town: old soldiers with rifles shouldered, the mayor with a few local dignitaries, the Marching Wildcats playing John Philip Sousa, all followed curiously by a group of Shriners on go-carts throwing candy. Apparently, the children lining the sidewalks also needed convincing that this was a worthwhile activity.

The River Falls Veterans Memorial is an imposing structure, a semi-circular wall of granite behind a row of flagpoles, benches for the dignitaries, and a central podium. The citizens of River Falls occupied lawn chairs on the green space, and countless others hovered around the peripheries. At the rear of the crowd was the band, directed to stand at attention through the ceremony. Along the street behind them stood a self-appointed honor guard, somber-looking men in leather uniforms bearing the insignia "Harley Riders for Christ."

The show began predictably with a local member of the clergy pronouncing God's blessing on America. The propaganda continued for about an hour and a half, the afternoon growing hotter, during which time three of the band students broke ranks by fainting and there was a clattering of trombones and tubas as their buddies frantically tried to catch their falling comrades.

Each veteran took the podium to relate his or her experiences. The World War II soldier spoke at great length of his time in Europe. My thoughts drifted, but I regained consciousness in time for his closing words: "Thank God we dropped the bomb on those Japs!" This horror was followed by testimony from veterans of the less justified wars, the final witness a young woman recently returned from Iraq to tell us of the glory of that adventure.

The preacher then blessed us all, and we walked home feeling totally ambivalent about our country and its confused citizenry. I couldn't help thinking what a different society we'd be if we spent this much money and time to honor those returning from the Peace Corps. God bless America indeed.

**Danny, Wish You Were Here**
**Bill Quist**

Remember when we were pirates
sailing haystacks through alfalfa
wind, and the meadowlarks singing?

Remember when I went to sea,
fell off the edge of the earth, returned
to find you flying, how far out you were?

Remember chances we took, tripping
without a net, to Dark Side of the Moon,
coming down on someone's lawn?

Remember when I came to shore and you
didn't, remember telling me once more
the same story you're telling me now?

Remember what it was like before
you began to fade, gliding our canoe
among sleeping pelicans at midnight?

Do you remember me now in a hayfield?
Remember how I loved you?

Cavity Lake Fire BWCAW

Richard Birger

### Meeting of the Waters
### Lisa Langsetmo

Here where 3 sisters stood
A storm of 4 nations came

I cannot ask why

Standing trees are silent
The fallen are missing
The earth is ruddy brown

Here where the spirit whispers
The roots grow to listen
Here where tears were given
Sweet water flows back

Here at the center of all things
No seekers shall find
But those who are lost
Will be home at last

So far I have travelled
That my soles have worn through

### Schadenfreude
### Lisa Langsetmo

I laugh
too quickly
perhaps
it is
not funny
at all

The medicine
I need
we need
is deeper
and more painful

The body politic
is wounded
the community
broken

We fight
each other

Act re-act
She
she is dying

Found Opera House                    Joe Schur

**COVID-Cut Ties**
**Mary E. Knatterud**

Scratching my head in perplexity,
it aches, quakes, with and for you:
this plague, this life, has sliced us all.
So why, why, excise me from your days,
cutting short our calls, curtailing our texts,
ghosting me electronically, emotionally,
in ambiguous (not cut-and-dried) ways,
inflicting heart-dicing paper cuts,
now red, angry, infected.
As my mom would cry, *Cut it out.*
I am not your scratch paper, to cuttingly ignore
or curtly blow off
or casually scissor to pieces
too jagged to write anything cogent on.

### Seventy-Five Miles from Paradise
### July 25, 2021
### Lia Rivamonte

When I was a 4th grader in Northern California, I won a poster contest sponsored by the local fire department; its theme and purpose: fire prevention. My drawing featured an iron resting atop an ironing board, plugged into an electric outlet. A circle of short lines radiated around the outlet to indicate energy. Today in certain parts of the world it takes far less than leaving an appliance plugged in to ignite a fire that will destroy acreage the size of a small country, reduce hundreds of structures to ash, and leave thousands of people and animals without shelter—whole communities vanished in a matter of hours. Global warming was never just a figure of speech, nor was it an idea for future consideration. The earth is burning beneath our feet; we suck in the residue from fires with every breath.

In July of this year, my daughter texted me a photo that had gone viral. It pictured the house she lived in two years ago. The house was ablaze, enveloped in flames. Located in Plumas County, California, in the upper northeast quadrant of the state, the house was seventy-five miles from the town of Paradise, devoured by fire in 2018. The rugged terrain includes Lassen Volcanic National Park, arguably the most beautiful park in a state that includes the likes of Yosemite, Joshua Tree, Sequoia, and Redwood National Parks.

White settlers claimed this land of the Maidu, Paiute, and Washoe people, somehow thinking to dignify this theft by referring to it as "Indian Country," hence the name of the unincorporated community of Indian Falls.

Many who choose to live in this part of the country among ancient-growth trees, giant boulders, and icy-clear, fast rivers seek isolation, preferring small town life or as few people as possible. Some are in pursuit of a less cluttered life, yearn for harmony with nature, and are committed to its protection; still others are armed to the teeth, wave Confederate flags, and are dedicated to the protection of their perceived personal rights.

A few days prior to the event that led to the photograph, I imagine someone stepping out the front door of the house, shivering slightly under the cool canopy of the feathery pines looming above. The brittle-brown pine needles crunch underfoot as they take a moment to inhale the perfume wafting from the trees. As children we learned to bury our noses into the deep-ridged bark of tall, wide pines to determine its type. "It's a Jefferson," the naturalist explained, "if it smells like vanilla."

As children we learned to draw houses resembling a box with a triangular roof, two windows, and a front door. If asked, it would have been easy to include flames. Moving the pencil in and out of the spear-shapes, varying the height of their tips, allowing them to curl just a little, suddenly it's a house on fire. The aftermath is much more complicated.

*Photo credit: Camille Swezy.*

*From the Archives*
**The Story Behind the Blue and White Banner**
**Shelley Butler**

Have you ever wondered where we acquired the beautiful art and artifacts at Unity? I've enjoyed the tall blue and white banner that hangs in the sanctuary from time to time for many years, not knowing anything about it until recently, when I learned that there is an interesting story behind it.

During the Vietnam War, tens of thousands of Hmong soldiers, an estimated one-fourth of all Hmong men and boys, fought alongside the United States in Laos and Vietnam. The U.S. signed a "peace treaty" in 1972, that called for the withdrawal of all foreign military troops from Laos, which expanded the power of the Communist Pathet Lao or Lao People's Liberation Army. A CIA officer said to those who had sided with the U.S., "If we lose, we will take care of you," according to the Hmong Timeline on the Minnesota Historical Society website.

In 1975, South Vietnam and Laos fell to Communist control. It was official: we lost. Hmong soldiers and families who worked with the CIA were at risk of being captured and/or killed by the Pathet Lao. At the Long Cheng air base, 30,000 Hmong families showed up to escape, but only 2,500 were actually airlifted to Thailand. Thousands more did manage to find their way out of Laos on their own.

That same year the first Hmong family resettled in Minnesota, but it wasn't until the U.S. Refugee Act of 1980 was passed that thousands more came; Minnesota is now proudly home to the largest population of Hmong in the United States.

In 1982, three members of the Social Concerns Group at Unity Church—Warner Shippee, Chip Peterson, and Jon Booth—organized the Indochinese Refugee Assistance Program (IRAP) to offer direct help and support to Hmong refugees. Many Unity members stepped up big time to help in a wide variety of ways, including hosting Hmong artisan sales and developing an appreciation for this art.

A record of activities of IRAP was kept on index cards and updated yearly. From the card labeled "Banner":

> In 1985, a committee was formed to commission a banner for the church. A design needed to be selected as well as colors and a Hmong artisan. In Spring 1986, Xiong Lee, an award-winning artist, was asked to create the banner which was presented to the congregation on September 14, 1986.
>
> Designed and sewn in the traditional Pa Ndau, IRAP sees the banner as a visual reminder to church members to learn about and better understand the people and cultures of the Indochinese refugees. IRAP seeks to express the U-U understanding that respect for the values and perceptions of other cultures most effectively assists new American adjust to our county.

Let this banner continue to be a reminder of our UU values and of Unity Church members who cherished Hmong American art and people.

Note: Pa Ndau is the sophisticated Hmong needlework art of reverse appliqué that has been adapted from ancient times. "Pandau" means "cloth made beautiful like a flower." From "A Story in Every Stitch" by Betty Lundy. *Chicago Tribune*, Dec 11, 1988.

Photo: "Xiong Lee at Unity Church Unitarian, St. Paul, Minnesota." Unity Church Unitarian, Accessed September 11, 2021. https://collection.mndigital.org/catalog/ p16022coll74:136

Indigenous Dancer at State Fair                          Carolyn Walkup

## Ode to a Goddess Yearning
### John David Wilson

Divine Goddess, you are both Beauty and Truth
As light is both particle and wave,
And perhaps so much more:
So too you appear in all these manifestations,
Yet retaining your mystery—
Alive as frequency and vibration.
Alive as the swirling Light of Reality, as Truth,
Beyond all our preconceived assumptions.

What can be said of spiritual Beauty?
Beyond all colors, forms and harmonies,
Yet dwelling at the center of each and every momentary appearance.
Beauty arises from your touch upon our lives and Consciousness.
Beauty arises, born in the pink of dawn;
Enduring all day and in the big brightness of stars.
Thus all the universe is adorned with your charm.

Come walk across the water
Gathering flowers of love that float
Above the suffering of the world.

As we fill these flower baskets,
Chanting songs of courage and love,
Preparing the altar of your inner aarti.

All the beings of your loving heart emerge:
Harmony transforms the universe
As Love dissolves all separation.

Here, in oppression, where suffering flows,
We walk across the muddy river of life
Without haste, fearlessly offering our love.

We gather souls in love, releasing all suffering;
Not lingering in ages of loss, but understanding
That we may name and thus tame these currents.

As your love draws the lotus to the sunlight,
Releasing all that suffering sticks to—floating free.

Hong Kong 2                                        Robert Gestner

*Story for All Ages*
**The Unfinished Journey**
**Rev. K.P. Hong**

A special good morning to the families and to the children who are joining us today. Children, I invite you to come a little closer... I'm going to imagine you a little closer as we join together for this morning's story.

At the end of *The Hobbit*, Bilbo Baggins ends up back home at Hobbiton. At the end of *The Wonderful Wizard of Oz*, Dorothy ends up back home in Kansas. And at the end of *A Wrinkle in Time*, the Murrays are back home in their small New England town. It seems that in all of these beloved stories of epic journeys, the heroes come back home at last.

And so also at the end of that great and ancient epic journey, *The Odyssey*, King Odysseus is back home with his family, back on his throne on the Greek island of Ithaca. But as he stands there, he's trying to remember something, something half-forgotten, that his journey is not quite over as there is one more leg of the journey he must take. Anyone who knows the story knows what a long and impossible journey it has been. Where had he been?

He had set out twenty long years before. The hero Odysseus had sailed away from home on the island of Ithaca to fight an unnecessary war against the people of Troy. The Trojan War went on for ten years with both sides wearing thin, until Odysseus, a master of disguise and deception, finally thought up an ingenious plan to deceive the Trojans. Odysseus had his Greek soldiers build a great wooden horse, knowing the horse was a sacred symbol for the people of Troy. When the Greeks then pretended to sail away, the Trojans pulled the horse into their city as a victory trophy. The Greeks were gone, and they could now celebrate! But Odysseus had secretly hidden his soldiers inside the wooden horse, and that night, the Greek warriors crept out of the horse and opened the city gates, letting in the Greek forces who had sailed back under the cover of night. They stormed the city and conquered the Trojans, winning the war.

After ten years of waging war against the Trojans, Odysseus set out on the dark sea and began his journey home. But his return voyage would take another ten long years, delayed by storms and shipwrecks, and it seemed he would never reach home. But if Odysseus knew anything, he knew how to sail and how to command others, and how to use disguise and deception to help him get out of all manner of difficulties. But while he was so clever and crafty in dealing with monsters and storms out in the world, he didn't know how to handle the monsters and the storms churning inside his own heart. He seemed so clever at disguise and deception, but struggled to be honest and true.

At one point, exhausted and broken from his journey and feeling all was lost, Odysseus found himself sailing through the underworld of Hades, haunted by the ghosts and souls of the dead. An oracle appears to Odysseus foretelling his homecoming, but that after reclaiming his throne, Odysseus must make one further journey. He finds the strength to pull himself out of Hades and, persevering through additional trials, he finally makes it home to Ithaca and fights off his rivals to reclaim his throne. He stands there, reunited with his wife and son and father, back on his throne on Ithaca. He has come home.

But just when the story seems like it has reached its glorious and appropriate ending, just when he can relax and enjoy his triumphs, Odysseus stands there trying to remember something half-forgotten, something that the oracle had told him: that the journey was not yet finished, that there was something more that the gods required of him.

"You must make a journey inland, Odysseus," the oracle had said. "You must carry your oar until you come to a people who know nothing of the sea, who have never tasted salt from the sea, who know nothing about ships and oars."

Just when Odysseus thought his journey had arrived at its final destination, he's called to journey inland from the outer island coast, from his small island into the larger mainland that lay beyond his map. Odysseus must walk and walk until he meets people who mistake his oar for a winnowing shovel, a farming tool used to scoop up grain and toss it into the wind to separate wheat from the outer shell. And there, Odysseus must bury his oar in the ground.

Only when Odysseus has traded in his oar for a winnowing shovel can his journey come to an end. His oar which has been his tool for survival. His oar with which he has steered his path. His oar that has been his identity and symbol of triumphs. Only when the old device is let go and reimagined as a winnowing shovel can his journey come to an end. A winnowing shovel for separating grain from chaff, what is useful from what is not, what is essential from what is nonessential. Only when the tool for maneuvering stormy seas has become a tool for discerning wisdom can Odysseus come to journey's end. Only then will he complete his travels, and only then will he truly return home.

For the journey was never about coming back to rule over his small island, but to connect with a world and people greater than just himself. To let go of being clever and learn to become wise.

And so may it be with our journeys.

Amen.

*This Story for All Ages was delivered during the service "Where to? What next?" on Sunday, August 30, 2020, at 10:00 a.m. To view the service, visit the Unity Church-Unitarian channel on YouTube, select the "Sunday Service" playlist, and scroll down to find the date and title: www.youtube.com/c/unitychurchunitarian.*

Thomas Heaton Homage                                    Richard Birger

## Contributors and Index

**Dutton Foster** retired from teaching English and drama, as well as directing and designing plays, for over forty years, and enjoys painting, writing, and construction projects ranging from model railroad structures to Habitat homes. He and Caroline enjoy birding, biking, and bluegrass, among other pastimes. Dutton is happy to be a member of the *Cairns* editorial staff. **Pages: 57, 73**

**Marcia Franklin** dabbled in two or three careers (to go with her two master's degrees) before settling into her role as chatelaine of the manor (and stay-at-home mom) in St. Paul with her husband and twin daughters. She writes fantasy and science fiction, and studies multiple languages for fun. **Page: viii**

**Robert Gestner** I am a retired 3M Chemist who enjoys taking vacation photographs. **Pages: 53, 98**

**Rebecca Gonzalez-Campoy** is a social justice volunteer at Unity Church-Unitarian and a second-year student at United Theological Seminary of the Twin Cities, pursuing a master of divinity in the social transformation track. Medical clinic administrator, parent of three adult children and two adult dogs, Becky lives in Sunfish Lake with husband, Mike. **Page: 36**

**Richard Hamer** Works and lives in Mendota Heights with wife, Donna. Has two grown children, Anna and William. Is a volunteer leader with SCORE, working to mentor persons of color who wish to start and run their own businesses. **Pages: 84, 85**

**Reverend Karen Hering** serves as associate minister at Unity Church and is the founder of the Faithful Words literary ministry. She is the author of *Writing to Wake the Soul*, and a new book, *Living in the Between: A Thresholder's Guide to Personal and Global Change*, to be published soon. **Page: 6**

**Reverend K.P. Hong** currently serves as the Minister of Faith Formation at Unity Church-Unitarian, where he's learning that children are masters at opening things: everything from crayon boxes to tubes of toothpaste to sacred words to national borders to racial categories to our sacred imagination. K.P. comes to ministry shaped by Korean Buddhism and Christianity, in the interreligiously religious condition and challenge of faith today. **Page: 99**

**Reverend Doctor Kathy Hurt** is serving as the Interim Minister of Unity this church year. She comes back to us with much experience, after serving as an intern and being ordained at Unity Church in the '80s, and then, serving as our Pre-interim Minister in 1999. Central to her ministry has been her focus on supporting and guiding the ongoing spiritual growth of individuals and groups, a focus that has been present in her writing, teaching, and preaching. **Page: 43**

**Mary E. Knatterud** Mary E. Knatterud is an independent writer-editor, recently retired from the University of Minnesota surgery department. The mother of three grown children, she lives in St. Paul with her husband, Jim Johnson. **Pages: 68, 91**

**Lisa Langsetmo** Minnesota native used to cold lonely winters. Writing poems line by line and tossing them into the ether. Dancing between joys and sorrows for the short time I am here. **Page: 90**

**Richard Lau** is originally from Honolulu, Hawaii, but decided twenty-three years ago that he wanted to experience -50 wind chill, and never left. He now lives in Woodbury with his wife, Heather, their two daughters, two dogs, and two cats. When not cooking, eating, talking about cooking or eating, teaching religious education, or being part of Unity's Multicultural Conversation Partners Group, Rich is a real estate attorney in private practice. **Page: 48**

**Gary Mabbott** practiced and taught analytical chemistry for over 45 years. Now he practices poetry, guitar, singing, and cooking. He sings in Unity Choir along with his wife, Ann. His son, granddaughter, and daughter-in-law live a short walk from them. **Pages: 18, 19**

**Reverend Shay MacKay** is our Coordinator of Community Outreach Ministries at Unity Church. She served as the Hallman Ministerial Intern in 2015-2016, and was ordained at Unity in 2017. In between, she did some chaplaincy work and served two small congregations in southern Maine. Shay believes her calling is one of discovery, expression, and celebration of the Spirit within the world and all people. **Pages: 8, 9**

**Hilary Magnuson** is a lifetime member of Unity Church, since 1941. She is a former elementary school teacher, and volunteers in the Unity Bookstall and at Obama School. **Page: 55**

**Carol Mahnke** I graduated from Concordia College in Moorhead, MN, in 1972, and later earned a master of liberal arts from Moorhead State University. I was a reporter for *The Forum* in Fargo, ND, in the 1970s and 1980s. When my husband, Terry, became a Lutheran (ELCA) pastor, we moved to Iowa where he served five parishes over almost twenty years. I became an emergency medical technician while we were in our last parish. He died in 2016, and I moved back to the Twin Cities where I grew up. I have two sons—one in Portland, OR, with my 10-year-old grandson, and another son and daughter-in-law in Roseville. **Page: 69**

**Neil Mikesell** I am a retired salesman & teacher. I have been privileged to have had my poetry published in *Cairns* previously. Lately I have been writing a few essays for a private project and this is one of them. **Page: 58**

**Barbara Nicholson** Barbara retired from the criminal justice system to find hope and beauty in the world around us. She published a book of poetry, *Reclamation,* in 2019. **Pages: 80, 81**

**Kathryn Oakley** Kathryn Oakley is a St. Paul writer, career consultant, and poet. She retired in 2015 from a long career in adult education and career guidance. Her collected poems, *Incense Drifting to the Horizon*, appeared in 2017 from North Star Press. She's been a member at Unity since 1991. **Page: 59, 64**

**Cynthia Orange** Cynthia Orange (www.cynthiaorange.net) is an author, freelance writer, editor, and writing consultant. She has won awards for essays, poetry, and journalism, and her most recent books, *Take Good Care: Finding Your Joy in Compassionate Caregiving* and *Shock Waves: A Practical Guide to Living with a Loved One's PTSD* both received national Nautilus Awards. She co-facilitates Unity's Caregiving Group. **Pages: 11, 74**

**Beth Peterson** Creating, whether through writing or in embroidery, helps me process and express my life more fully. I am grateful to be in a writing group through Unity. I am also grateful my Mom taught me to embroider at a young age and that it continues to bring me joy and solace. **Page: 35**

**Bill Quist** grew up in South Dakota, spent four years in the Navy, six years in college, and thirty years as a poet trapped in an engineer's body. His poems have appeared in *Cairns, Passager, Wisconsin People & Ideas, Red Booth Review, Poetry Jumps Off the Shelf, Wisconsin Poets Calendar*, and more obscure places. His chapbook manuscript *Shape of a Hole* was runner-up in the 2019 Heartland Review chapbook contest and a semi-finalist in the 2020 Eggtooth Editions contest. His website is www.billquistpoet.com. **Pages: 87, 88**

**Lia Rivamonte** lives in the Little Bohemia neighborhood of St. Paul, MN, with her husband, Matt Brown. Her poetry chapbook, *Tell Me When You Get There*, was published in 2019 by Finishing Line Press. She has been the recipient of a MSAB Artist Initiative grant, and a Metro Regional Art Council Next Step grant. She is currently (and forever) nursing a novel and other writing projects. **Page: 92**

**Molly Rodich** I'm a high school student who likes to take pictures of things I think look interesting to me. One day we were on the bus and the sun hit my friend's eye in an interesting way, so I took the picture with my phone. **Page: 31**

**Natasha Rodich** One of the few born-and-raised Unitarians, I feel lucky to stop on occasion and see the world through the camera lens. **Page: 83**

**Paul Rogne** Starting as a child, I was always fascinated by photography—taking pictures, looking at those my father took, learning to develop and print in our basement darkroom. Now I use a digital camera and computer to do the same tasks—

that is just much quicker and more flexible. I find that the best photo-opportunities are the ones that happen when I have my camera along. Some are unexpected, when I just look down, up, or turn away from what I originally was looking and aiming at. **Pages: 38-39, 76**

**Amanda Rueter** Amanda Rueter has her PhD in personality psychology and has a BA in Fine Art. She spends much of her time as a brain researcher at the University of Minnesota and an adjunct professor at St. Catherine University. In her free time, she enjoys gardening, gathering her chickens' eggs and feeding them veggies, and taking her dog on walks. **Pages: 7, 21**

**Joe Schur** I enjoy rambling about taking photographs, mostly on my iPhone now. My recent work includes nature themes as well as man-made artifacts and structures. **Pages: 47, 52, 91**

**Kathy Schur** My art medium is primarily watercolor, which I find challenging, but highly rewarding in its versatility and beauty. I am a signature member of the Minnesota Watercolor Society. **Pages: cover, 10, 12**

**Linny Mae Siems** The roller-coaster ride I am on continues. My challenge to stay in the moment is an on-going choice. I pray, "Please" and "Thank You," every day. **Page: 13**

**Cynthia Starkweather-Nelson** Most of my life has been spent as a practicing artist: teaching, painting, drawing, printmaking, and exhibiting my work whenever and wherever possible. My work is a response to the visual inspirations I encounter in this amazing world. I have been a member of Unity Church since the early '80s and enjoy staying connected in many ways, virtually, as a resident of Tucson, AZ. **Page: 51**

**Daphne Thompson** Daphne likes to write family history memoir-style. **Pages: 60, 62, 82**

**Jane Thomson** I have worked in the arts all my adult life, as a painter or in another capacity. When in March 2020 the pandemic first appeared here, not having a car, my son and his family began taking me on walks in parks that I had never been to before. Woods, water, and family were sanity-savers and inspired some nature paintings. **Page: 86**

**Carolyn Walkup** I began doing photography in my youth with a simple box camera and went on to use Nikons with many lenses, especially when I traveled. Today my cell phone camera is proving to be my camera of choice whenever I see something I want to record. **Page: 96**

**Bill E. Webb** As a drummer and singer my entire adult life, I am often reminded of life's many rhythms that surround us in the world. Those rhythms often become word play for me. This poem was in response to a creative writing class while attending United Theological Seminary. **Page: 16**

**Arlene West** As I turn away from my business of graphic design, I am lucky to spend time with and appreciate our grandchildren and my mother. It is a refreshing new chapter. **Page: 56**

**John David Wilson** I have studied/done meditation for over 50 years; thus, my poems tend to the mystic. Preferring to live in the Present, poems note the qualities of the Now, without attachment. Who writes? The inner Consciousness. **Page: 97**

**Peggy Wright** I paint impressionistic landscapes and waterscapes because I want to focus on color and texture, not realistic details. I want to show the essence of the emotions that I experience when I participate in nature: a love of its beauty and a feeling of connection with the plants and animals around me. Playing with color and texture is my passion, and I use hue, texture, and form to explore the world. **Pages: 42, 63**

**Colophon**

While *Cairns* is set in Lucida Bright, a font praised for its clarity, we also add a little extra line spacing so your eyes have more room to work.

*Cairns* is printed using an on-demand printing service. Each copy costs a little more than if we printed a lot of them at once, but the paper, glue, and ink are only used for books that people actually want. We're grateful you wanted one!

Made in the USA
Monee, IL
04 December 2021